The 5 Ingredients or Less
Low Carb Slow Cooker Cookbook
For Rapid Weight Loss And Overall Health

Top **100** Quick, Easy and Flavored Crock Pot Recipes for Smart People

By Adam Jain

Disclaimer

Table of Contents

About The Book

Are you fed up with your overweight? Are you looking for a diet for weight loss? Do you want to have delicious foods without paying too much time everyday? If yes, then this book is right for you! It is not just a cookbook, it is a complete guide of Low Carb diet. It is a perfect companion for your daily cooking!

So what benefits will you get by following a low carb diet?
1. Helps In a Swift Reduction In Appetite.
2. Helps To Lose Weight Effectively.
3. Lowers The Blood Triglycerides.
4. Increases The Levels Of Good Cholesterol (Hdl).
5. Reduces The Blood Sugar Levels.
6. Reduces Hypertension.
7. Helps Improve Brain Disorders.
8. Gives More Energy.
9. Improves Health And Fitness.
10. More And More...

Besides, by following this book, you will know:
1. Everything About Low Carb Diet;
2. Foods You Should Eat/ Avoid
3. Why Slow Cooker;
4. 100 Delicious And Easy Slow Cooker Recipes
5. More and more...

Out there in our world today, we see a lot of overweight people, in churches, our workplaces, grocery stores and so on. Most of them often do make attempt towards fighting the weight problem, but often a times do fail. What most of them obviously always fail to know is that, for anyone to see a positive result in weight loss, you have to follow a good and efficient diet plan alongside a proper exercise routine. One of the most productive methods of losing weight is through adopting a certain diet plan. Many people follow numerous diet plans, hoping to lose weight, but still fail to get their dream body just because they adopt the wrong kind of diet plan. So, if you are in search of an effective dieting remedy, that will help you lose a great deal of weight and invariably keep you healthy, fit, and active, regain confidence, then this book is certainly for you.

For some people, weight loss could be very tedious, but the truth is, it's not that much of a stress. Anyone can lose weight, have a sexy looking bikini body and live a healthy lifestyle. The only thing needed is for one to be precise, because weight loss processes are more about addressing the key issues in an appropriate manner, so that the weight will be under control by the person and at the same time won't have to leave the person worrying about being overweight or losing control.

The main aim of this book is to help people lose weight, regain confidence and stay fit permanently by introducing them into a low carb diet plan. The book also provides solutions to all the matters concerning weight loss. And most essentially, all the recipes included in this book will make you have a taste of healthy and tasty foods that will invariably nourish your body. If you are sick and tired of following unsuccessful diet plans that at the end of the day amount to nothing, then this book is all you could ever ask for.

The book contains 100 delicious and mouthwatering low carb slow cooker recipes. If you're a busy person who finds it hard to carve out time to prepare meals, then you can take advantage of slow cooker to save time, fuel and energy.

Meantime, all of these recipes are well chosen and proven to be top recipes. All you need to do is just buy the ingredients in your local market and put them into the slow cooker, then wait for some hours you will have a very nutritional and mouth-watering dish. Hope you will like this book and get the benefits you want!

N/B: All the recipes are made from natural, organic, low carb, and whole foods. So, let the journey begin.

Introduction

The book "The 5 Ingredients or Less Low Carb Slow Cooker Cookbook For Rapid Weight Loss And Overall Health- Top 100 Quick, Easy and Flavored Crock Pot Recipes for Smart People" is a cookbook that targets people who wish to have a taste of some easy, delicious and healthy low carb slow cooker recipes for the purpose of weight loss and living a healthier lifestyle.

Unarguably a low carb diet helps you to stay in shape without adding extra pounds to your body. Obesity is one of the biggest issues faced by millions of people around the world. When it comes to weight loss and diet, many people feel unmotivated and get frustrated just by thinking of it. So, if you are struggling to lose some pounds of weight or want to live a much healthier lifestyle, then this cookbook is for you. Low Carb diet is an effective and natural way of eating with low carb high fat foods.

Having a fixed diet plan and exercising sounds very easy, but the hardest part is in implementing them, because that is where the real work is. And so with that, we aim at main making people understand the effectiveness of low Carb intake in the process of weight loss. Many people believe that the higher the percentage of fat in their diet the more likely they are to having serious health issues like obesity, heart disease and much more. While this may be true, as many studies have recommended that people should reduce their intake of fat by less than 30 percent in total, still notwithstanding it is advisable even by many health professionals to make use of a Low Carb Diet plan to ensure better health, weight loss, and fitness. Many studies conducted in recent years have shown the effectiveness of the low Carb diet over many other diet plans. The main outcome measurements were in cholesterol level, obesity, blood sugar, and Triglycerides. These studies were conducted on people having health problems, which included obesity, type II diabetes, and metabolic syndrome.

The first study was conducted by **Foster GD, et al.** a randomly selected trial of a low-carbohydrate diet for obesity . **New England Journal of Medicine, 2003.** This study had about 63 individuals on a low Carb diet for 12 months. The results however showed a 7.3% loss of total body weight in the patients. Moreover, the patients had greater improvement in their blood triglycerides and HDL. (http://www.nejm.org/doi/full/10.1056/NEJMoa022207)

10

The second study was conducted by Samaha FF, et al. a low-carbohydrate diet in comparison with a low-fat diet in tackling severe obesity. **New England Journal of Medicine, 2003.The study lasted** for 6 months, and at the end about 132 individuals with severe obesity were recommended the low Carb diet. Many of the individuals following the diet were having metabolic syndrome or type II diabetes as well.
(http://www.nejm.org/doi/full/10.1056/NEJMoa022637)

The study results showed that:
1. Triglycerides went down by 38 mg/DL.
2. Insulin sensitivity improved very prominently.
3. Fasting Blood sugar went down by 26 mg/DL.
4. Insulin went down by 27%.

Also in 2012 a study was carried out by Guldbrand, et al. Concerning a type 2 diabetes, a comparison was made between a randomly selected group of people who were advised to follow a low-carbohydrate diet as it transiently improves Glycaemic and a group advised to follow just a low-fat diet producing a similar weight loss. **Diabetologia, 2012.** The results showed that the low Carb group had greater reductions in BMI and other biomarker improvements.
(https://link.springer.com/article/10.1007%2Fs00125-012-2567-4)

So in a nutshell, if you want a flat stomach, reduction in weight, regain confidence, and to live a healthier life then this book will actually be your savior.

Essentials You Need To Know

If you are a busy person, it could be frustrating at most times as you will often find yourself not being able to do carryout some certain tasks like having enough time to prepare meals that will maintain your weight and glucose level in a good way. Well if you are among such group of persons, then I am glad to announce to you that there is finally a way out of this frustration as this book will reduce the whole processes to its simplest and quickest form, and improve your health condition provided you follow the low carb diet properly. In today's fast and changing society, we all get busy at some point and do need meals that are healthy and easy to prepare. For us, the solution is hidden in junk food choices which are not healthy enough to keep us fit. All the junk foods, artificial flavors, and processed food items are the major causes of bad health and obesity, which often do leads to severe disease like heart attack, diabetes, headache, kidney stones, etc.

Nowadays, millions of people in the world are suffering from obesity, hypertension, and diabetes. The sickness worsens when proper care and attention to address it are not available which often results in life threatening diseases .Taking all that into account, it is highly recommended to have the low Carb diet plan as it does not only guard you off this fatal diseases but also reduces your weight and blood sugar. The Low Carb diet plan is the most efficient method to all the obese people, as well as those who want to lose some extra pounds. The plan includes low Carb fruits, vegetables, meat, fish, poultry, nuts, and unsweetened items. Before we proceed, let us clear the air on what the Low Carb Diet is.

What Is A Low Carb Diet?

This is a very simple diet plan that limits the carbohydrates found in most of the starchy fruits, vegetables, and grains. The main emphasis is on food with high protein, fiber, and fat.

History of the Low Carb Diet

The history of this diet goes back to 1972 when a cardiologist named Robert C. Atkins created a diet plan that restricted carbs while emphasizing on protein and fat. His basic purpose in creating this plan was to change an eating habit to enhance good health, weight loss, and fitness. According to Dr. Atkins, this diet is a healthy lifelong approach to eating. It helps maintain weight, cholesterol, sugar level, and blood pressure.

The Health Benefits of the Low Carb Diet

Some proven benefits of the low Carb diet plan are:
•   Low Carb diet lowers the hunger pangs in a good way. It helps in a swift reduction in appetite.
•   Eating fewer calories help to lose weight effectively.
•   Blood triglycerides are fat molecules in blood and are known for causing heart diseases. Low Carb diets effectively lower the blood triglycerides.
•   Increases the levels of Good Cholesterol (HDL).
•   Reduces the blood sugar levels.
•   Reduces hypertension.
•   Helps improve brain disorders.
•   Gives more energy.
•   Improves health and fitness.

Permitted and Non Permitted Foods in the Low Carb Diet Plan

Non Permitted
Bread and grains, Sugar breakfast cereal, Starchy fruits
Starchy vegetables, Beer, White sugar, Maple syrup
Honey, Agave nectar, Sweetened yogurt, Milk

Permitted
Unsweetened almond milk, Unsweetened coconut milk
Small amount of lentils and beans, Olive oil, Nut oil

Vinegar, Low Carb fruits, Low Carb Vegetables
Meat, Eggs, Natural yogurt, Small amount of wheat

How Can Low Carb Diet Enhances Weight loss

The low Carb diet is all about cutting Carbs from the meal, invariably causing your kidney to start shedding excess water. From the water loss most people lose a lot of weight at the start which is actually water weight that reaches up to 5-10 pounds. After the first week, it will then focus on shredding fat from your fat stores. The low Carb diet helps in reducing ones appetite and invariably causing weight loss without the need for calories control. So that means you can eat as much as you wish to and still feel satisfied as well. In addition, the low Carb diet also helps in reducing the insulin level which store fats in the body, and by so doing leading to a reduction in the body weight.

23 Tips to Attaining a Successful Low Carb Diet Plan

Along with a healthy low Carb diet plan, timing is the most important factor. First, it is important to know the type of meal you want to prepare. If you follow a proper meal plan, it will surely have a significant effect on your overall health. Another important thing that you will need to take care of is the timing of when you will be eating your meal. Eat properly and on time as it will help speed up your metabolism rate more effectively, and prevent the body from increasing its fat storage.

1. Reduce the amount of added sugar and other carbs in your meal.
2. Calculate your Carbs percentage using a handy crab counter.
3. Keep calories as low as possible, because too much will slow down the weight loss process.
4. Eat regularly and keep starvation at bay.
5. Include protein in your everyday meal.
6. Eat more vegetables and fruits.
7. Drink a good amount of water.
8. Enjoy drinking tea or coffee, as it both helps in getting rid of water weight.
9. Take a daily multivitamin supplement.
10. Indulge yourself in any physical activity and exercise.

11. Keep track of your success on a diet.

12. Decide on your choices of meal before shopping in the grocery.

13. Eat breakfast as early as possible after waking up.

14. Appreciate personal food choices as well. There is no need to go hard on any diet.

15. Check the food labels before buying any food item for extra sugar content.

16. Go for organic food items.

17. Avoid artificial flavors and preservatives.

18. Say a big "NO" to sodas and canned juices while on the low Carb diet. You can substitute these beverages with healthy homemade smoothies and juice made from low Carb vegetable and fruits.

19. Concentrate more on leafy vegetable, low Carb fruits, vegetables, fish and white meat based meal plans.

20. Chose the healthiest oil for cooking that is cholesterol free.

21. Consume a low Carb, high protein, and a high fiber diet.

22. Go low on overall carbohydrates.

23. Always fill half your plate with fruits and vegetables.

Frequently Asked Question

1. How many Carb one should eat on low Carb diet?
The Institute of Medicine recommends a dietary allowance of carbohydrate at 70 grams daily for 2000 calorie meal plan.

2. Can you drink coffee or tea while on a low Carb diet?
Yes, but keep added sugar at bay.

3. Can you eat nuts on the low Carb Diet?
Not in the first week.

4. Can a vegan follow low Carb diet?
Yes, it can be followed by vegan or vegetarians.

5. Can lentil be part of a low Carb diet?
Yes, but in limit.

Who Should Partake in the Low Carb Diet

Adding less Carb in one's daily meal can make a huge difference to your overall health. It helps in reducing weight, lowering insulin level, kidney disease and much more. The low Carb diet is strongly recommended for:

1. People with diabetes
2. People with kidney diseases
3. People with obesity
4. People with any sort of inflammation
5. Older and middle age people
6. People with hypertension

The Challenges Faced When Following a Low Carb Diet

When following the low Carb diet plan the most common challenges that most of us are likely to face are:

- The Family eating at different times
- The differences in food choices
- Redundant meal menu
- Medical needs
- Life philosophy needs
- Budget and time

It is important for one to develop the willpower to resist all the sweet treats and high Carb meals. It's important to always keep in mind the overall calorie intake. The core practice of eating healthy in low Carb meals is the pyramid to an optimal fitness and health.

CAUTION

All the recipes that are included in our meal plan responds differently to each and every individual, so it's best to consult your doctor before starting a low Carb diet. From time to time visit your doctor to monitor the changes in your blood sugar and weight.

Low Carb Diet Hacks

Below are some low Carb diet hacks, which help you to choose some basic ingredients to start a meal plan.

**Swap these food items**	_**For these food items**_
Sodas and juices	Milk, water and lemon
Burger and French fries	Salads and bun less burgers
Toast and sandwich s	Lettuces wrap and egg wraps
Snacks	Meat, vegetables, and cheese
Processed meat	Organic meat
Ice-cream	Organic and natural yogurt or cakes
Sweets	Chocolate
Cocktail	Red wine
Flour	Almond flour or coconut flour
Crumbs	Grounded Almonds
Margarine	Butter or ghee
Icing	Cream cheese frosting
Sugar	Stevia
Potatoes	Cauliflower
Jam	Berries or fruits
Rice	Cauliflower rice
Processed yogurt	Natural yogurt
Cereal	Eggs, bacon
Milk	Nut milk
Frozen meal	Fresh food items
High Carb fruits	Low Carb Fruits
High Carb vegetables	Low Carb vegetables

8 Low Carb Diet Myths

Despite being a successful plan for effective weight loss and a healthy lifestyle, there are numerous amounts of misconceptions and myths about low Carb diet.

Some people believe that low Carb diet is a complete human diet plan and that one should adopt it for better health. While many others think that it is a "fad" diet which is not suitable for human beings due to the adverse effect it has on the body on the long run. Here is the list of the most common myths.

1. It Is a Known as a Fad Diet Plan

The word fad has a lot of meanings. Most people use it to tag a diet plan that they do not deem as being efficient. The low Carb diet was used as a weight loss diet plan, which enjoyed a short popularity; and as such today, a lot of people label the low Carb diet a fad diet. Logically this is erroneous, as there are numerous studies carried out in the past that shows the effectiveness of this diet. It is a well-known & approved diet plan that is being adopted by millions of people for decades now. If we carry out a research about the diet, we will find out that in 1863, a book was published solely for it that sold a million copies worldwide. It is a diet plan that has been in existence for a while now and has been supported by many health professionals, by so doing countering the erroneous tag of it being a Fad diet.

2. It Is Difficult To Follow

Many people are of the view that it is a very difficult diet to follow as it restricts commonly found food items from being consumed. This makes people feel uncomfortable, causing them to abandon the low Carb diet, which often ends in weight gaining still. While this maybe a reasonable argument, it is important to note that almost all the diet plan restricts food items. Some restrict fat, some strict macro nutrients, and others limit calories. The good thing about the low-Carb diet is that it reduces hunger, so that you can still eat until you are satisfied and invariably manage to lose weight at the same time.

3. The Weight You Lose Is Water Weight Not Fats

The human body stores a lot of carbs in the liver and muscle called glycogen. Glycogen is used to provide glucose to the body which also helps in binding some certain percentage of water. When you stop eating carbs, this storage drops, and your body in turn loses water weight. The low-Carb diet causes reduction in insulin levels which results in making the kidney to lose excess of amount of water and sodium. That single mechanism is the reason why it leads to a reduction in water weight. In addition, the studies suggest that this diet also leads to the reduction in fat, especially from the liver and abdomen.

4. Low-Carb Diet Is Bad For the Heart

The Low-Carb diets are high in fat and low in carbs. Many of us think that they are detrimental to the heart. However, many studies have shown that fat or cholesterol has no adverse effect on the heart functions.

5. Low-Carb Diets Is Successful Because We Eat Lesser Calories
Many of us believe that when we eat less, we lose weight easily; this is only true to some extent. But on a low-Carb diet, weight loss happens almost instantaneously. We feel much fuller and satiated, that we eat less without counting the calories intake. The art of reduction in appetite in the low-carb diet serves as the most effective method to restricting calories intake. And also it is important to note that the Low-Carb diets digestion benefits goes far beyond the calories.

6. It Reduces Our Plant Food Intake
It is a misconception, that reducing Carb makes you eat fewer plant foods. In reality, you can eat a lot of vegetables, nuts, berries, and seeds. But remember, not to exceed 50 g per day.

7. The Brain Needs Glucose
Many people are of the notion that the brain cannot work properly without carbs and that the brain needs 130 grams of carbs each day to function properly. While this is partially true because some brain cells do need glucose to get proactive, that notwithstanding the other parts of the brain are solely dependent on the ketones to get active. If carbohydrates are in short supply, then a significant part of the brain uses ketones instead of glucose. So, here the metabolic track known as gluconeogenesis gets imported where it produces glucose from protein.

8. It Affects Our Physical Performance
Many sportsmen and athletes eat high-Carb diet meal and are healthy. The reduction in Carbs can lead to low performance, of which will only last temporarily until the body gets used to it with time.

Why Slow Cooker?

From the title of the book you will know this book is about low carb diet slow cooker, that means almost all of these recipes are made in slow cooker or Crock-pot. Why we use slow cooker for low carb dieting?

Firstly, the slow-cooker is an economical, electrical cooking appliance that cooks food at low temperature using the simmering method. **It is not expensive, all of us can have one!**

Secondly, Slow-cooking requires minimal effort, as the food is cooked over a low heat, unattended, for many hours. **It is very easy to use and save you too much time!** All you have to do is place your prepared ingredients into the slow-cooker, switch it on, set the heat settings, and then do anything else you want to. Your meal will be waiting for you after some hours. Could it be any easier?

Thirdly, the slow-cooker is the perfect cooking utensil for cooking many different dishes, such as soups, stews and pot roasts – foods that can cook slowly for many hours.

Fourthly, Using a slow-cooker reduces the use of multiple cooking utensils, and as the food is cooked at a low temperature, there is no danger of burning it.

Finally, the most important is that the foods will be very delicious and nutritional after some hours slow cooking. Slow cooking softens the connective tissues in meat, which makes the foods more nutritional!

So now we know some knowledge of low carb diet and slow cooker, it's time to go into the recipe part! Let's go on!

Low-Carb Chicken Recipes

1. Salsa Verde Chicken

Ingredients

- 6 chicken breasts, boneless
- 2 teaspoons ground cumin
- salt and ground black pepper as needed
- 2 cups Salsa Verde
- 12 fl oz chicken broth

Instructions

- Season the chicken with ¼ teaspoon each of salt and black pepper, then place in a 4-quart slow-cooker.
- Pour in the chicken broth, and top with the Salsa Verde.
- Stir until all the ingredients are well-combined.
- Cover and seal the slow-cooker with the lid, set the cooking timer for 4 hours, and allow to cook on a high heat setting.
- When cooked, remove the chicken and shred the meat with forks.
- Mix the meat into the cooking liquid, and serve in a lettuce wrap.

Servings: 6

Nutritional Information Per Serving:

Energy: 264 Kcal
Carbohydrates: 5.4 g
Net Carbs: 4.4 g
Fats: 11.1 g
Protein: 34.3 g

2. Ranch Chicken Taco Lettuce Wraps

Ingredients

- 12 oz chicken breasts, boneless
- 2 tablespoons taco seasoning
- 2 tablespoons ranch seasoning, dried
- 2 tablespoons apple cider vinegar
- 3 tablespoons olive oil

Instructions

- Place all of the ingredients in a 4-quart slow-cooker, mixing well.
- Ensure that the slow-cooker is sealed with the lid, set the cooking timer for 6 to 8 hours, and allow to cook on a low heat setting.
- After cooking, shred the meat with forks, then toss back into the cooking liquid.
- Serve immediately, wrapped in lettuce.

Servings: 4

Nutritional Information Per Serving:

Energy: 434 Kcal
Carbohydrates: 10.9 g
Net Carbs: 6.7 g
Fats: 13.5 g
Protein: 27.7 g

3. Chicken with Green Beans

Ingredients

- 12 oz chicken breast, boneless
- 30 oz fresh green beans, trimmed
- 2 teaspoons ground cumin
- 2 cups Salsa Verde
- 6 cups chicken broth

Instructions

- Place all of the ingredients, apart from the green beans, in a 4-quart slow-cooker, stirring together until the chicken is coated.
- Cover the slow-cooker with the lid, set the timer for 3 hours, and allow to cook at a low heat setting.
- Add the beans, and allow to continue cooking for another hour.
- Shred the chicken with forks, then toss back into the cooking liquid, mixing well.
- Serve immediately.

Servings: 4

Nutritional Information Per Serving:
Energy: 481 Kcal
Carbohydrates: 5 g
Net Carbs: 4 g
Fats: 30 g
Protein: 39 g

4. Lemon Garlic Chicken

Ingredients

- 24 - 30 oz whole chicken
- 2 heads of garlic, halved (add more if preferred)
- 4 lemons, seeded and halved (add more if preferred)
- 1 rosemary sprig
- 2 tablespoons all-purpose steak seasoning

Instructions

- Place the half of both the garlic and the lemon halves, cut side down, at the bottom of a 4-quart slow-cooker. Place the rosemary sprig on top.
- Stuff the chicken with the remaining lemon and garlic heads, sprinkle with steak seasoning, then place it on top of the ingredients in the slow-cooker.
- If you like stronger flavors, you can place any additional lemon and garlic on top of the chicken at this point.
- Seal the slow-cooker with the lid, and set the cooking timer for 4 hours, allowing the chicken to cook at a high heat setting.
- Remove the chicken from the slow-cooker and carve.
- Strain the cooking liquid from the slow-cooker and serve it alongside the chicken.

Servings: 4

Nutritional Information Per Serving:
Energy: 673 Kcal
Carbohydrates: 10.18 g
Net Carbs: 7.68 g
Fats: 46.82 g
Protein: 51.86 g

5. Cheesy Barbecue Chicken

Ingredients

- 4 chicken breasts
- 2 cups Hot Barbecue Sauce, low-carb and sugar-free
- 4 ounce shredded sharp cheddar cheese
- Salt and black pepper to taste

Instructions

- Place the chicken breasts in a 4-quart slow-cooker.
- Cover with the barbecue sauce, season with salt and black pepper, then seal the slow-cooker with its lid.
- Set the cooking timer for 3 hours at a high heat setting.
- Sprinkle with cheese, and allow to continue to cook for 15 minutes at a high heat setting, until the cheese melts completely.
- Serve straight away.

Servings: 4

Nutritional Information Per Serving:
Energy: 293 Kcal
Carbohydrates: 6 g
Net Carbs: 5 g
Fats: 17.8 g
Protein: 29.5 g

6. Five-Spice Chicken Wings

Ingredients

- 16 chicken wings
- 3/4 cup plum sauce, sugar-free
- 1 tablespoon unsalted butter, melted
- 1 teaspoon Chinese five-spice powder, organic if possible
- Salt and black pepper to taste

Instructions

- Set oven to 375F and allow to preheat.
- Remove and discard wing tips.
- Line a large baking sheet with aluminum foil and spread the chicken wings across it in a single layer.
- Season with salt and black pepper to taste, then place the baking tray in the oven and bake for 20 minutes.
- In the meantime, place the remaining ingredients in a 4-quart slow-cooker and mix until they are well combined.
- When chicken wings begin to color, drain away any liquid, then add them to the slow-cooker.
- Ensure that the chicken wings are well-coated with the liquid ingredients, then seal the slow-cooker with its lid.
- Set the slow-cooker to cook at a low heat setting for 4 hours.
- Serve warm.

Servings: 2

Nutritional Information Per Serving:
Energy: 186 Kcal
Carbohydrates: 0.2 g
Net Carbs: 0.1 g
Fats: 18.7 g
Protein: 21.4 g

7. Hoisin Chicken

Ingredients

- 12 chicken thighs, skinless
- 6 oz broccoli (thawed if frozen)
- 2 tablespoons tapioca
- Salt and ground black pepper to taste
- 1/2 cup peanut butter hoisin sauce, sugar-free

Instructions

- Lightly grease the bottom and inner sides of a 4-quart slow-cooker with a non-stick cooking spray, then place the chicken thighs in it.
- Sprinkle with tapioca and a pinch of salt and ground black pepper.
- Top with the hoisin sauce, and seal the slow-cooker with its lid.
- Allow to cook at a low heat setting for 4 to 5 hours.
- Stir in the broccoli, and continue to cook for 30 to 45 minutes on a high heat.
- Serve with cooked cauliflower rice.

Servings: 6

Nutritional Information Per Serving:
Energy: 100 Kcal
Carbohydrates: 0.5 g
Net Carbs: 0.25 g
Fats: 8.5 g
Protein: 11.1 g

8. Chicken Coconut Curry

Ingredients

- 15 large chicken thighs, skinless
- 1 medium red onion, peeled and sliced
- 1 ½ teaspoons minced garlic and 1 teaspoon grated ginger
- 2 teaspoons curry powder, organic if possible
- 1 cup coconut milk, full-fat

Instructions

- Grease the bottom and inner sides of a 4-quart slow-cooker with a non-stick cooking spray and then place the sliced onion inside.
- Top with the chicken thighs, and sprinkle with a pinch of salt and ground black pepper.
- In a separate bowl, mix together the coconut milk and curry powder, and pour this mixture over the chicken.
- Seal the slow-cooker with its lid, and allow to cook for 3 to 3 1/2 hours at a high heat setting.
- Remove the chicken thighs, then remove the meat from the bones, and cut into bite-size pieces.
- Return the chicken to the slow-cooker, and stir gently into the cooking liquid.
- Serve with bread or cooked cauliflower rice.

Servings: 5

Nutritional Information Per Serving:

Energy: 353.8 Kcal
Carbohydrates: 6.2 g
Net Carbs: 5.6 g
Fats: 29 g
Protein: 26.4 g

9. Cranberry Chicken

Ingredients

- 4 chicken thighs, skinless and de-boned
- 1 cup cranberries, fresh (you could use defrosted frozen berries)
- 1/4 cup tomato ketchup, organic if possible
- 2 tablespoons coconut sugar
- 2 teaspoons Dijon mustard

Instructions

- Grease the bottom and inner sides of a 4-quart slow-cooker with a non-stick cooking spray, and place the cranberries inside.
- Place the chicken thighs on top.
- In a separate bowl, mix the remaining ingredients together, then pour this mixture over the chicken.
- Seal the slow-cooker with its lid, and allow to cook for 6 ½ to 7 ½ hours at a low heat setting.
- Serve warm with cooked cauliflower rice.

Servings: 4

Nutritional Information Per Serving:
Energy: 170.6 Kcal
Carbohydrates: 8.6 g
Net Carbs: 7 g
Fats: 28 g
Protein: 25.7 g

10.   Chicken Noodle Soup

Ingredients

- 2 chicken breasts
- 4 medium carrots, peeled and chopped into bite-sized pieces
- 1/2 cup bean sprouts
- 2 cups spiralized squash noodles
- 6 cups chicken stock

Instructions

- Grease the bottom and inner sides of a 4-quart slow-cooker with a non-stick cooking spray, and add all of the ingredients apart from the noodles.
- Season with a pinch of salt and ground black pepper, then seal the slow-cooker with its lid.
- Set the cooking timer for 6 to 8 hours, and allow to cook on a low heat.
- Remove the cooked chicken, and shred with forks.
- Return the shredded chicken to the slow-cooker, add the noodles, and continue cooking for 20 minutes on a low heat.
- Garnish the soup with herbs, and serve piping hot.

Servings: 6

Nutritional Information Per Serving:
Energy: 154 Kcal
Carbohydrates: 8.2 g
Net Carbs: 5.3 g
Fats: 14.4 g
Protein: 1.7 g

11.   Chicken Fajitas

Ingredients

- 6 chicken breasts
- 2 red onions, peeled and sliced
- 3 bell peppers, in any color, de-seeded and sliced
- 2 tablespoons fajita seasoning,
- 1/2 cup chicken broth

Instructions

- Grease the bottom and inner sides of a 4-quart slow-cooker with a non-stick cooking spray.
- Place the onion and the bell peppers at the base of the slow-cooker, place the chicken breasts on top, and pour in the chicken broth.
- Cover and seal slow-cooker with its lid, and set the cooking timer for 3 to 4 hours.
- Allow to cook at a high heat setting.
- Shred the chicken with forks, and mix back into the vegetable mixture.
- Serve with lettuce wraps, and your favorite toppings alongside.

Servings: 6

Nutritional Information Per Serving:
Energy: 417 Kcal
Carbohydrates: 13 g
Net Carbs: 5.6 g
Fats: 29.1 g
Protein: 27.3 g

12.   Spinach Artichoke Chicken

Ingredients

- 12 oz chicken breast, diced
- 5 oz fresh baby spinach (you could use thawed, frozen spinach)
- 6 oz artichoke hearts, chopped
- 4 oz cream cheese
- 4 oz shredded cheddar cheese

Instructions

- Grease the bottom and inner sides of a 4-quart slow-cooker with a non-stick cooking spray and place the chicken inside.
- Add the cream cheese, half of the cheddar cheese, and the artichoke hearts to the chicken, mixing all of the ingredients together.
- Cover the slow-cooker with the lid, setting the cooking timer for 4 hours, and allow to cook at a high heat setting.
- Add the spinach, and allow to cook for a further 20 minutes.
- Sprinkle the remaining cheddar cheese over your cooked ingredients, and continue to cook for 5 minutes or until cheese is completely melted.
- Serve hot.

Servings: 4

Nutritional Information Per Serving:
Energy: 240.1 Kcal
Carbohydrates: 17.6 g
Net Carbs: 14.6 g
Fats: 5.1 g
Protein: 30.5 g

13. Apple Cider Pulled Chicken

Ingredients

- 8 oz chicken breasts, diced
- 2 tablespoons Italian seasoning
- 1 cup apple cider vinaigrette dressing

Instructions

- Grease the bottom and inner sides of a 4-quart slow-cooker with a non-stick cooking spray.
- Rub the Italian seasoning evenly over the chicken pieces, then place them in the slow-cooker.
- Pour over most of the dressing, holding back 2 tablespoons.
- Cover and seal slow-cooker with the lid, and allow to cook for 4 to 5 hours at a high heat setting.
- To serve, remove the chicken from the cooking liquid, and drizzle with the remaining dressing.

Servings: 3

Nutritional Information Per Serving:
Energy: 223 Kcal
Carbohydrates: 0 g
Net Carbs: 0 g
Fats: 7 g
Protein: 40 g

14.   Korean Pulled Chicken

Ingredients

- 4 chicken breasts
- 1 teaspoon minced garlic and 1 tablespoon grated ginger
- 1/3 cup erythritol
- 2 tablespoons soy sauce
- 1/4 cup tomato paste

Instructions

- Grease the bottom and inner sides of a 4-quart slow-cooker with a non-stick cooking spray, and place the chicken breasts inside.
- Mix together remaining ingredients, then pour this mixture over the chicken.
- Seal the slow-cooker with the lid, and set the cooking time for 4 hours at a high heat setting.
- Remove the chicken, shred it with forks, return it to the cooking liquid, and mix gently.
- Serve with shredded lettuce.

Servings: 4

Nutritional Information Per Serving:
Energy: 510 Kcal
Carbohydrates: 5.6 g
Net Carbs: 2.3g
Fats: 30 g
Protein: 51.5 g

15.   Chicken and Broccoli Alfredo

Ingredients

- 2 chicken breasts
- 4 oz broccoli (you could use thawed, frozen broccoli)
- 4 oz cauliflower florets
- Salt and pepper
- 15 oz Alfredo sauce, low-carb

Instructions

- Grease the bottom and inner sides of a 4-quart slow-cooker with a non-stick cooking spray and place the chicken inside.
- Season with a pinch of salt and black pepper, and then the remaining ingredients.
- Cover the slow-cooker with its lid, set the cooking timer for 3 hours, allowing it to cook on a low heat setting.
- Shred the chicken with forks, and return it to the cooking liquid, mixing well.
- Garnish with grated mozzarella cheese and serve hot.

Servings: 2

Nutritional Information Per Serving:
Energy: 416 Kcal
Carbohydrates: 4.1g
Net Carbs: 3 g
Fats: 24 g
Protein: 45.6 g

Low-Carb Lamb Recipes

1. Lamb Curry

Ingredients

- 1 lb diced lamb
- 6 oz fresh baby spinach
- 5 teaspoons curry powder
- 15-ounces marinara sauce, sugar-free
- 1/2 cup water

Instructions

- Place a medium-sized skillet over medium heat, grease with oil and add the diced lamb.
- Stir in the curry powder, and a pinch of salt, and cook gently for 7 to 10 minutes, or until golden brown.
- Transfer the meat into a 4-quart slow-cooker.
- Stir in the marinara sauce and the water, ensuring the meat is fully immersed in the liquid.
- Cover and seal the slow-cooker, allowing the food to cook for 3 hours at a high heat setting.
- Stir in the spinach leaves and continue cooking for another half hour, or until the spinach is tender.
- Serve warm with cauliflower rice.

Servings: 4

Nutritional Information Per Serving:
Energy: 310 Kcal
Carbohydrates: 5 g
Net Carbs: 4 g
Fats: 17 g
Protein: 33 g

2. Lamb and Green Beans

Ingredients

- 3 lb lamb leg, on the bone
- 6 cups fresh green beans, trimmed
- 4 cloves of garlic, peeled and sliced
- 2 tablespoons dried mint
- 2 cups of chicken broth or water

Instructions

- Season the lamb on all sides with salt and black pepper.
- Place a large skillet over a medium heat, allow 2 tablespoons of butter to melt, then add the seasoned lamb.
- Allow to brown, turning frequently, to ensure that it is golden brown on all sides. This should take 10 – 15 minutes.
- Transfer the lamb to the slow-cooker, sprinkle with the garlic and mint, and add the water.
- Cover the slow-cooker with the lid, and allow the lamb to cook for 6 hours at a high heat setting.
- Check occasionally and if the lamb gets dry, pour in an additional 1/2 cup of water.
- Place the beans into the slow-cooker, and allow to continue cooking for another hour. The beans should be tender-crisp.
- Serve hot, although the leftover meat can also be enjoyed cold.

Servings: 4

Nutritional Information Per Serving:
Energy: 525 Kcal
Carbohydrates: 12 g
Net Carbs: 7.4 g
Fats: 36.4 g
Protein: 37.3 g

3. Lamb Shoulder

Ingredients

- 1 lamb shoulder, on the bone
- 2 tablespoons mixed herbs
- 1/4 teaspoon xanthan gum
- 2 cups chicken stock, warmed

Instructions

- Grease a 4-quarts slow-cooker with a non-stick cooking spray.
- Season the lamb with the mixed herbs and a pinch of salt and pepper, and place it in the slow-cooker.
- Pour over the stock, and seal the slow-cooker with its lid. Set the cooking timer for 7 to 8 hours, and allow the meat to cook on a low heat setting, or until the meat is tender.
- When the lamb is cooked to your liking, transfer it to a plate and keep warm.
- Transfer the cooking liquid into a saucepan, stir in the xanthan gum and allow to cook gently until the gravy has reduced to the desired thickness.
- Carve the meat into slices, and serve with a jug of gravy alongside.

Servings: 4

Nutritional Information Per Serving:
Energy: 488 Kcal
Carbohydrates: 1 g
Net Carbs: 1 g
Fats: 36 g
Protein: 39 g

4. Cinnamon Lamb

Ingredients

- 2 lb lamb shoulder, diced
- 4 tomatoes, chopped
- 2 cloves of garlic, minced
- 1 tablespoon ground cinnamon
- 1 large bunch of coriander

Instructions

- Place the lamb in a 4-quart slow-cooker.
- Add the tomatoes, garlic, cinnamon, a pinch of salt and pepper, and pour in 1/2 cup water.
- Cut off the stalks from the coriander bunch and add these.
- Cover the slow-cooker with the lid, and set the cooking time for 5 hours, at a low heat setting.
- After this time, roughly chop the coriander leaves, and add them to the slow-cooker, allowing a further 20 minutes of cooking time at a high heat setting.
- Serve with cauliflower rice.

Servings: 4

Nutritional Information Per Serving:

Energy: 352 Kcal
Carbohydrates: 4 g
Net Carbs: 2.8 g
Fats: 27 g
Protein: 39 g

5. Lamb Stew

Ingredients

- 8 lamb shoulder chops, trimmed and cut into bite-sized pieces
- 8 oz turnips and/or carrots, peeled and chopped
- 8 oz mushrooms, sliced
- 2 garlic cloves, minced
- 2 cups beef broth, warmed

Instructions

- Grease a 4-quarts slow-cooker with a non-stick cooking spray and place all of the ingredients inside, adding a pinch of salt and pepper.
- Cover and seal slow-cooker with its lid, and allow to cook for 6 hours on a low heat setting.
- Transfer the stew to a serving platter, with all of the cooking juices, garnish with mint leaves, and serve.

Servings: 4

Nutritional Information Per Serving:
Energy: 405 Kcal
Carbohydrates: 13 g
Net Carbs: 9.7 g
Fats: 18.9 g
Protein: 53 g

6. Lamb with Onions and Thyme

Ingredients

- 6 lb leg of lamb
- 4 large white onions, peeled and diced
- small bunch thyme sprigs
- 1/2 cup parsley leaves
- 10 fl oz red wine

Instructions

- Season the leg of lamb with a pinch of salt and black pepper.
- Place a large skillet over a medium heat, and add 2 tablespoons of oil.
- Allow the lamb to turn golden-brown on all sides, turning frequently for about 15 minutes.
- Transfer the lamb onto a plate and add the onions into the pan.
- Allow to cook gently for 10 minutes, until the onions are soft and lightly browned.
- Spoon onion mixture into a 4-quart slow-cooker, then add the lamb, the wine, and the herbs.
- Seal the slow-cooker with its lid, and allow to cook on a high heat for 4 hours.
- Garnish with thyme sprigs to serve.

Servings: 4

Nutritional Information Per Serving:
Energy: 183 Kcal
Carbohydrates: 3 g
Net Carbs: 2.6 g
Fats: 12 g
Protein: 19 g

7. Lamb with Edamame Beans and Tomatoes

Ingredients

- 12 oz ground lamb
- 1 cup frozen edamame beans, thawed
- 3 cups diced tomatoes,
- 1 tablespoon minced garlic
- 2 teaspoons curry powder,

Instructions

- Grease a 4-quarts slow-cooker with a non-stick cooking spray and place all of the ingredients inside.
- Season with salt to taste, then stir in 1 1/2 cups of water.
- Cover the slow-cooker with its lid, and allow the food to cook for 5 to 6 hours at a low heat setting.
- Pour into warmed bowls, and serve immediately.

Servings: 8

Nutritional Information Per Serving:
Energy: 243.4 Kcal
Carbohydrates: 13.8 g
Net Carbs: 9.6 g
Fats: 15.4 g
Protein: 38.4 g

8. Mustard Lamb

Ingredients

- 12 lamb shoulder chops, trimmed
- 1/4 cup Dijon mustard
- 1 cup raw honey
- 1/2 cup chicken stock

Instructions

- Grease a 4-quarts slow-cooker with a non-stick cooking spray and place the lamb chops inside.
- Stir the remaining ingredients together in a bowl, until mixed well, and pour this mixture over the lamb chops.
- Cover the slow-cooker with its lid, and set the cooking timer for 4 to 5 hours, allowing to cook at a high heat setting.
- Serve immediately.

Servings: 6

Nutritional Information Per Serving:
Energy: 153 Kcal
Carbohydrates: 2 g
Net Carbs: 2 g
Fats: 4 g
Protein: 26 g

9. Sweet and Spicy Lamb

Ingredients

- 12 lamb shoulder chops, trimmed and cut into bite-sized pieces
- 1 medium-sized white onion, peeled and chopped
- 2 garlic cloves, minced
- 1/8 teaspoon xanthan gum
- 1 cup sweet and sour sauce, low-carb and sugar-free
- 3/4 cup hot barbecue sauce, low-carb and sugar-free

Instructions

- Grease a 4-quart slow-cooker with a non-stick cooking spray.
- Place the meat pieces, onion, garlic and sauces into the slow-cooker, and cover it with the lid.
- Allow to cook for 4 to 5 hours at a high heat setting.
- Stir in xanthan gum, and continue cooking for 10 to 15 minutes, until the sauce thickens to the desired consistency.
- Serve warm with cooked cauliflower rice.

Servings: 6

Nutritional Information Per Serving:
Energy: 166.1 Kcal
Carbohydrates: 0.9 g
Net Carbs: 0.9 g
Fats: 6.3 g
Protein: 23.9 g

10.   Chinese Style Lamb Shoulder

Ingredients

- 3 lb lamb shoulder
- 5 carrots, peeled and cut into chunks
- 1 large white onion, peeled and chopped
- 1/4 cup minced ginger
- 2 teaspoons Chinese five spice powder, and 2 tablespoons soy sauce

Instructions

- Place the onion, ginger, and carrots in a 4-quart slow-cooker.
- Mix the soy sauce and the Chinese five spice powder together, then rub this mixture over the lamb shoulder.
- Place the lamb on top of the vegetables in the slow-cooker, and place the lid on the slow-cooker.
- Allow to cook for 3 to 4 hours at a high heat setting.
- Serve the cooked vegetables alongside the lamb.

Servings: 4

Nutritional Information Per Serving:

Energy: 412.8 Kcal
Carbohydrates: 5 g
Net Carbs: 4.7 g
Fats: 20.9 g
Protein: 44 g

Low-Carb Beef Recipes

1. Steak Pizzaiola

Ingredients

- 12 oz flank steak
- 1 sweet bell pepper, de-seeded and sliced
- 2 tablespoons Italian seasoning
- 12 oz pasta sauce, sugar-free
- 4 oz shredded mozzarella cheese

Instructions

- Grease a 4-quart slow-cooker with a non-stick cooking spray.
- Season the beef with salt, ground black pepper, and Italian seasoning, place in the slow cooker, then pour in the pasta sauce.
- Top with peppers and cover the slow-cooker with its lid.
- Set the cooking timer for 6 to 8 hours, and allow to cook at a low heat setting.
- Remove the beef, and keep warm. Add the mozzarella to the slow-cooker, allowing to melt, but cooking for a further 20 minutes.
- To serve, slice the beef, and serve alongside the tomato mixture.

Servings: 4

Nutritional Information Per Serving:
Energy: 211 Kcal
Carbohydrates: 4 g
Net Carbs: 3.6 g
Fats: 9.4 g
Protein: 26.3 g

2. Sweet and Spicy Meatballs

Ingredients

- 12 oz meatballs
- 14 oz chili sauce, sugar-free
- 12 oz raspberry jam, sugar-free

Instructions

- Grease a 4-quart slow-cooker with a non-stick cooking spray, and place the meatballs inside.
- Stir the chili sauce and the jam together in a bowl, then add to the slow-cooker.
- Cover the slow-cooker with its lid, and set the cooking timer for 8 hours, allowing to cook at a low heat setting.
- Serve with cauliflower rice.

Servings: 4

Nutritional Information Per Serving:
Energy: 92 Kcal
Carbohydrates: 4.5 g
Net Carbs: 3.9 g
Fats: 5.1 g
Protein: 7 g

3. Beef Ragu

Ingredients

- 12 oz beef short ribs, trimmed and cut into chunks
- 1 cup white onion, peeled and sliced
- 4 cups chopped tomatoes
- 3 tablespoons tomato paste, sugar-free
- 1 teaspoon dried basil and dried oregano

Instructions

- Season the beef with salt and ground black pepper.
- Place a large skillet over a medium heat, add a tablespoon of olive oil, then add the beef pieces.
- Allow to cook for 4 to 5 minutes, turning until all sides are seared.
- Grease a 4-quart slow-cooker with a non-stick cooking spray and add the remaining ingredients, mixing well.
- Add the seared beef pieces, and place the lid on the slow-cooker.
- Allow to cook for 6 to 8 hours at a low heat setting.
- Shred the beef with forks, and return it to the cooking liquid. Allow it to sit for 15 minutes.
- Garnish with grated cheese, and serve with zucchini noodles.

Servings: 8

Nutritional Information Per Serving:

Energy: 513.4 Kcal
Carbohydrates: 12.4 g
Net Carbs: 9.2 g
Fats: 29.7 g
Protein: 45.8 g

4. Corned Beef and Cabbage

Ingredients

- 6 lb corned beef brisket
- 4 medium-sized carrots, peeled and cut into bite-size pieces
- 8 cups shredded cabbage
- 1 corned beef spiced packet
- 6 cups water

Instructions

- Rub the meat with the corned beef spice packet.
- Grease a 4-quart slow-cooker with a non-stick cooking spray and add the carrots and the cabbage.
- Pour in water, then top with the seasoned beef.
- Cover the slow-cooker with its lid, and set the cooking timer for 6 hours allowing to cook at a low heat .
- Serve the meat immediately, with the vegetables alongside.

Servings: 12

Nutritional Information Per Serving:
Energy: 334 Kcal
Carbohydrates: 8.1 g
Net Carbs: 5.5 g
Fats: 22.8 g
Protein: 24.7 g

5. Ancho-Beef Stew

Ingredients

- 8 oz boneless beef chuck pot roast, trimmed
- 16 oz low-carb vegetables
- 1 tablespoon ground ancho-chile pepper
- 12 oz tomato salsa, sugar-free
- 1 1/2 cups of beef broth

Instructions

- Cut meat into bite-size pieces and season on all sides with the ancho-chile pepper.
- Place a large non-stick skillet pan over medium-high heat, add 1 tablespoon olive oil, then the seasoned beef.
- Allow to cook for 5 to 7 minutes, or until browned on all sides. Depending on the size of your pan, you can cook the beef chunks in batches.
- Grease a 4-quart slow-cooker with a non-stick cooking spray and add the vegetables.
- Top with the browned meat and season with salt and ground black pepper.
- Stir in the tomato salsa and the beef broth, then cover the slow-cooker with its lid.
- Set the cooking timer for 8 to 10 hours, allowing the meat to cook at a low heat setting or until meat is cooked through.
- Serve the meat warm, with the vegetables alongside.

Servings: 4

Nutritional Information Per Serving:
Energy: 288 Kcal
Carbohydrates: 8 g
Net Carbs: 6 g
Fats: 20 g
Protein: 20 g

6. Cider Braised Beef Pot Roast

Ingredients

- 8 oz boneless chuck pot roast, trimmed
- 1/2 cup chopped white onion
- 1 teaspoon garlic powder
- 1/4 cup apple cider vinegar
- 1/4 teaspoon xanthan gum

Instructions

- Season the chuck roast with the garlic powder, salt, and ground black pepper.
- Place a large non-stick skillet pan over medium-high heat, add a tablespoon of olive oil, then add the meat.
- Allow to cook for 7 to 10 minutes, turning until it has browned on all sides.
- Grease a 4-quart slow-cooker with a non-stick cooking spray and add the browned meat.
- Top with the onion and pour in the vinegar and 1 1/2 cups of water.
- Cover the slow-cooker with its lid, and set the cooking timer for 8 hours, allowing the meat to cook at a low heat setting.
- Place the meat on a plate, then shred using forks, and keep warm.
- Transfer the remaining mixture to a saucepan, add the xanthan gum, and bring to boil, allowing to cook until sauce reduces to the desired thickness.
- Serve the meat with the sauce alongside.

Servings: 4

Nutritional Information Per Serving:
Energy: 393 Kcal
Carbohydrates: 4 g
Net Carbs: 3 g
Fats: 28 g
Protein: 30 g

7. Cajun Pot Roast

Ingredients

- 18 oz boneless beef chuck roast, trimmed
- 1 white onion, peeled and chopped
- 14 oz diced tomatoes with garlic,
- 1 tablespoon Cajun seasoning,
- 1 teaspoon Tabasco sauce

Instructions

- Season the beef on all sides with the Cajun seasoning mix.
- Grease a 4-quart slow-cooker with a non-stick cooking spray, add the seasoned beef, and top with the onion.
- In a bowl, stir together the tomato with garlic, the Tabasco sauce and a pinch of salt and ground black pepper.
- Pour the tomato mixture over the vegetables and beef, then cover the slow-cooker with its lid.
- Set the cooking timer for 6 to 8 hours, and allow to cook at a low heat setting.
- To serve, transfer the beef to a serving platter, then top with onion and tomato mixture.

Servings: 8

Nutritional Information Per Serving:

Energy: 314 Kcal
Carbohydrates: 10.4 g
Net Carbs: 8.2 g
Fats: 15.1 g
Protein: 38 g

8. Sloppy Joes

Ingredients

- 1 lb ground beef
- 2 tablespoons Worcestershire sauce
- 1 tablespoon Dijon mustard
- 1 cup Picante Sauce, sugar-free
- 3/4 cup hot barbecue sauce, sugar-free

Instructions

- Place a large non-stick skillet pan over medium-high heat, and add the beef.
- Cook for 8 to 10 minutes, stirring regularly, until the meat is no longer pink.
- Drain the fat from the mixture, and transfer to a 4-quart slow-cooker.
- Stir in the remaining ingredients, and season with salt and black pepper.
- Seal the slow-cooker with its lid, then set the cooking timer for 6 to 8 hours, allow the mixture to cook at a low heat setting.
- To serve, place a generous helping of the mixture on a roasted Portobello mushroom caps, and top with a second Portobello mushroom cap.

Servings: 6

Nutritional Information Per Serving:

Energy: 162.5 Kcal
Carbohydrates: 2.5 g
Net Carbs: 2.5 g
Fats: 4.5 g
Protein: 24 g

9. Moroccan Beef Lettuce Wraps

Ingredients

- 12 oz beef roast, trimmed and cut into bite-size pieces
- 1 cup sliced white onions
- 1 teaspoon sea salt
- 4 tablespoons garam masala,
- 10 large lettuce leaves, for wrapping

Instructions

- Grease a 4-quart slow-cooker and add all the ingredients apart from the lettuce.
- Cover and seal slow-cooker with its lid.
- Set the cooking timer for 8 hours and allow to cook at a low heat setting.
- Remove the beef, and shred it using forks. Place the meat back in the slow-cooker, and continue cooking for another 2 hours.
- Serve warm, wrapped in the lettuce leaves.

Servings: 4

Nutritional Information Per Serving:
Energy: 209 Kcal
Carbohydrates: 0.7 g
Net Carbs: 0.7 g
Fats: 9.5 g
Protein: 30.4 g

10.   Steak Fajitas

Ingredients

- 16 oz flank steak
- 1 red and 1 green bell pepper, de-seeded and sliced
- 1 white onion, peeled and sliced
- 2 tablespoons fajita seasoning,
- 20 oz tomato salsa, sugar-free

Instructions

- Grease a 4-quart slow-cooker with a non-stick cooking spray and then pour the salsa in.
- Place the peppers and onion on top, and sprinkle with the fajita seasoning.
- Stir until mixed well, then cover and seal the slow-cooker with its lid.
- Set the cooking timer for 3 to 4 hours, and allow to cook at a high heat setting.
- Serve with shredded cheese and sour cream.

Servings: 4

Nutritional Information Per Serving:

Energy: 222 Kcal
Carbohydrates: 5 g
Net Carbs: 4 g
Fats: 12 g
Protein: 23 g

11.   Beef and Eggplant

Ingredients

- 2 lb ground beef
- 3 cans of chopped tomatoes
- 2 medium-sized eggplants, de-stemmed
- 3 tablespoons Lebanese Spice Blend
- 2 cups shredded mozzarella cheese

Instructions

- Cut the eggplant into large chunks and add to a 4-quart slow-cooker, greased with non-stick cooking spray.
- Stir together the ground beef and the spice blend, and season with salt and ground black pepper. Place this over the eggplant.
- Pour over the chopped tomato, then place the lid on the slow-cooker.
- Set the cooking timer for 4 hours and allow to cook at a low heat setting.
- Add the shredded mozzarella, and allow to cook for a further 30 minutes, until the cheese is melted.
- Garnish with parsley to serve.

Servings: 6

Nutritional Information Per Serving:

Energy: 209 Kcal
Carbohydrates: 8.1 g
Net Carbs: 7.4 g
Fats: 12.8 g
Protein: 15.9 g

12.   Barbecue Pulled Beef

Ingredients

- 12 oz beef pot roast, trimmed and cut into bite sized pieces
- 1 teaspoon minced garlic
- 1 teaspoon onion powder
- 1/4 cup apple cider vinegar
- 3/4 cup tomato ketchup, sugar-free

Instructions

- Grease a 4-quart slow-cooker with a non-stick cooking spray.
- Mix together all of the ingredients, apart from the beef, and place the mixture in the slow-cooker.
- Add the beef pieces, and season with a pinch of salt and ground black pepper.
- Cover and seal the slow-cooker with its lid, setting the cooking timer for 4 hours, and allowing to cook at a high heat setting.
- Shred the meat with forks, and serve between roasted Portobello mushroom caps.

Servings: 4

Nutritional Information Per Serving:
Energy: 380 Kcal
Carbohydrates: 6 g
Net Carbs: 5.2 g
Fats: 15 g
Protein: 49 g

13.   Chili with Beef

Ingredients

- 1 lb ground beef
- 2 cans diced tomatoes with green chilies
- 2 white onions, diced
- 4 garlic cloves, minced
- 1 1/2 tablespoon Mexican seasoning
- 6 oz tomato paste

Instructions

- Place a large skillet pan over medium-high heat, add the beef, half of both the garlic and the onion, and a pinch of salt and ground black pepper.
- Cook for 5 to 7 minutes, stirring regularly, until the meat is nicely golden brown.
- Drain off the fat, and add to the slow-cooker.
- Stir in remaining ingredients, and place the lid on the slow-cooker.
- Set the cooking timer for 6 to 8 hours, and allow to cook at a low heat setting.
- To serve, allow people to help themselves to cilantro, grated cheese and sour cream.

Servings: 6

Nutritional Information Per Serving:
Energy: 306 Kcal
Carbohydrates: 13 g
Net Carbs: 10 g
Fats: 18 g
Protein: 23 g

14.   Beef and Sweet Potato Massaman

Ingredients

- 3 lb beef roast, cut into large pieces, and coated with coconut flour
- 12 oz sweet potato, peeled and cut into bite-size pieces
- 2 red onions, peeled and sliced
- 1/2 cup Massaman curry powder
- 1 can full-fat coconut cream

Instructions

- Grease a 4-quarts slow-cooker with a non-stick cooking spray, and place all of the ingredients inside, stirring until mixed.
- Add 2 cups of water or chicken broth, mixing this through evenly.
- Seal the slow-cooker with its lid, and set the cooking timer for 8 hours, allowing the food to cook at a low heat setting.
- Remove the meat, and shred with forks, then transfer to the serving dish.
- Top with the onions and sweet potatoes, drizzle with the sauce, and garnish with coriander.
- Serve with cooked cauliflower rice.

Servings: 6

Nutritional Information Per Serving:
Energy: 256 Kcal
Carbohydrates: 2 g
Net Carbs: 1.1 g
Fats: 14.1 g
Protein: 29.1 g

15.   Stuffed Tomatoes with Meat and Cheese

Ingredients

- 12 oz sausagemeat
- 6 plum tomatoes
- 2 cans tomatoes with basil
- 3 tablespoons Italian seasoning
- 1 1/4 cup grated Monterey Jack cheese

Instructions

- Cut a thin slice from the top end of each tomato, then use a spoon to remove the seeds.
- Mix together the sausagemeat, the Italian seasoning, and a pinch of salt and ground black pepper, then fill each tomato with the meat mixture.
- Sprinkle each one with cheese.
- Grease a 4-quarts slow-cooker with a non-stick cooking spray and pour in the tomatoes with basil.
- Arrange the stuffed tomatoes on top, then place the lid on the slow-cooker.
- Set the cooking timer for 4 hours, allowing the food to cook on a low heat setting.
- Serve warm.

Servings: 6

Nutritional Information Per Serving:
Energy: 286 Kcal
Carbohydrates: 7.9 g
Net Carbs: 6.4 g
Fats: 23.3 g
Protein: 18.7 g

Low-Carb Turkey Recipes

1. Stuffed Peppers

Ingredients

- 6 oz ground turkey
- 4 small green bell peppers, with the tops cut off and deseeded
- 1 white onion, peeled and diced finely
- 1/2 teaspoon minced garlic
- 1 tin tomato pasta sauce, sugar-free

Instructions

- Place the ground turkey in a large bowl, and add the onion, garlic, and 2 tablespoon of tomato pasta sauce.
- Stir until well-mixed, and carefully stuff this mixture into the peppers.
- Grease a 4-quart slow-cooker with a non-stick cooking spray and place the remaining tomato pasta sauce in it.
- Place the peppers on top of the sauce, then seal the slow-cooker with its lid.
- Allow to cook for 6 to 8 hours on a low heat setting.
- Serve warm.

Servings: 4

Nutritional Information Per Serving:
Energy: 243 Kcal
Carbohydrates: 10 g
Net Carbs: 7 g
Fats: 14 g
Protein: 21 g

2. Ginger Turkey Lettuce Wraps

Ingredients

- 24-ounce turkey thighs, skinless
- 16 ounce shredded broccoli
- 3/4 cup sliced green onions
- 1 cup sesame-ginger sauce, low-carb and sugar-free
- 1/4 cup water

Instructions

- Grease a 4-quart slow-cooker with a non-stick cooking spray and then place the turkey in it.
- In a bowl whisk together sesame-ginger sauce and water until combined and then pour this mixture over turkey.
- Cover and seal slow-cooker with its lid, then plug in and set the cooking timer for 3 to 3 1/2 hours Allow to cook at a high heat setting or until meat is cooked through.
- When done, transfer turkey to a cutting board and let cool slightly.
- Then using forks and knife, separate meat and bones, discard the bones.
- Shred meat and return to the slow-cooker.
- Stir in broccoli, then cover and let stand for 5 minutes.
- To serve, place turkey mixture on top of lettuce, top with green onion and drizzle with sauce.
- Wrap and serve.

Servings: 12

Nutritional Information Per Serving:

Energy: 430 Kcal
Carbohydrates: 4 g
Net Carbs: 3 g
Fats: 19 g
Protein: 54 g

3. Shepherd's Pie

Ingredients

- 12 oz ground turkey
- 2 cups carrots, peeled and chopped
- 2 cups frozen peas, thawed
- 20 oz mashed cauliflower
- 2 tablespoons tomato paste, sugar-free

Instructions

- Grease a 4-quart slow-cooker with a non-stick cooking spray, add the ground turkey, carrots, peas, tomato paste and 1/3 cup water.
- Season with salt and ground black pepper and stir until mixed.
- Cover and seal slow-cooker with its lid, and set the cooking timer for 6 to 8 hours. Allow to cook at a high heat setting or until cooked through.
- Top evenly with mashed cauliflower, return to the slow-cooker, and continue to cook for 30 minutes.
- Serve warm.

Servings: 4

Nutritional Information Per Serving:
Energy: 303 Kcal
Carbohydrates: 4.1 g
Net Carbs: 2.3 g
Fats: 21.2 g
Protein: 21.5 g

4. Cranberry Turkey

Ingredients

- 1 large turkey breast
- 2 tablespoons dry onion soup mix
- 16 oz cranberry sauce, low-carb and sugar-free

Instructions

- Grease a 4-quart slow-cooker with a non-stick cooking spray and place the turkey breast inside.
- Sprinkle with onion soup mix and top evenly with the cranberry sauce.
- Cover and seal slow-cooker with its lid, set the cooking timer for 2 hours, and allow to cook on a high heat setting.
- Switch the heat setting, to low and continue to cook for a further 4 to 5 hours.
- Slice the turkey, and serve with the sauce alongside.

Servings: 4

Nutritional Information Per Serving:
Energy: 325 Kcal
Carbohydrates: 1.8 g
Net Carbs: 1.2 g
Fats: 5.8 g
Protein: 34 g

5. Ground Turkey and Mushrooms

Ingredients

- 6 oz ground turkey
- 1/2 cup chopped green onions
- 6 oz white mushrooms, sliced
- 1/4 cup beef gravy mix
- 1/2 cup water

Instructions

- Grease a 4-quart slow-cooker with a non-stick cooking spray and add the ground turkey.
- Stir in the mushrooms, gravy mix, and water, and mix until well-combined.
- Cover and seal slow-cooker with its lid, then set the cooking timer for 2 to 3 hours. Allow to cook at a high heat setting.
- To serve, season with salt and ground black pepper, and garnish with green onions.
- Serve in lettuce wraps.

Servings: 2

Nutritional Information Per Serving:
Energy: 314.1 Kcal
Carbohydrates: 0.5 g
Net Carbs: 0.4 g
Fats: 24.7 g
Protein: 20.5 g

6. Turkey Chili

Ingredients

- 1 ½ lb ground turkey
- 1 large white onion, peeled and chopped
- 1 ½ lb diced fire-roasted tomatoes with green chilies
- 14 oz tomato puree
- 6 cups beef broth

Instructions

- Place a large non-stick skillet pan over medium heat, add the ground turkey and allow to cook for 5 minutes, until nicely browned on all sides.
- Drain off the grease, and transfer the meat to a 4-quart slow-cooker.
- Stir in remaining ingredients, and season with a pinch of salt, ground black pepper and red chili powder.
- Cover and seal the slow-cooker with its lid.
- Set the cooking timer for 8 hours, and allow to cook on a low heat setting.
- Garnish with cilantro to serve.

Servings: 12

Nutritional Information Per Serving:
Energy: 311 Kcal
Carbohydrates: 12 g
Net Carbs: 9.1 g
Fats: 14.4 g
Protein: 33.7 g

7. Turkey Taco Meat

Ingredients

- 6 oz lean ground turkey
- 1 cup diced white onion
- 1 1/2 tablespoons Mexican-seasoning blend
- 2 tablespoons soy sauce
- 4 oz tomato sauce, low-carb and sugar-free

Instructions

- Grease a 4-quart slow-cooker with a non-stick cooking spray and add all of the ingredients.
- Season with a pinch of salt and ground black pepper.
- Cover and seal the slow-cooker with its lid, and set the cooking timer for 4 to 5 hours. Allow to cook at a low heat setting.
- Garnish with chopped green onion and serve in lettuce wraps.

Servings: 4

Nutritional Information Per Serving:
Energy: 255 Kcal
Carbohydrates: 6 g
Net Carbs: 4 g
Fats: 11 g
Protein: 30 g

8. Thai Turkey Legs

Ingredients

- 2 turkey legs, medium-sized
- 1 lime, halved
- 2 1/2 teaspoon lemon- garlic seasoning
- 15 oz coconut milk, full-fat

Instructions

- Pour the coconut milk into a 4-quart slow-cooker and stir in lemon-garlic seasoning.
- Juice one half of the lime, and stir the juice into the slow-cooker.
- Slice the other half of lime, and add to the slow-cooker.
- Add the turkey legs, cover and seal the slow-cooker with its lid.
- Set the cooking timer for 3 to 4 hours, and allow to cook at a high heat setting.
- Carve the meat from the bone, and serve warm.

Servings: 4

Nutritional Information Per Serving:
Energy: 275.8 Kcal
Carbohydrates: 4 g
Net Carbs: 2.8 g
Fats: 12.4 g
Protein: 35.5 g

9. Turkey Breast

Ingredients

- 4 lb turkey breast
- 2 tablespoons dry onion soup mix
- 6 tablespoons unsalted butter

Instructions

- Grease a 6-quart slow-cooker with a non-stick cooking spray, and place the turkey breast to it.
- Sprinkle with the dry onion soup mix, and then spread the butter on top.
- Cover and seal slow-cooker with its lid, and set the cooking timer for 10 hours. Allow to cook at a low heat setting.
- Gently transfer turkey to the serving platter, cover, and let allow to rest for 10 minutes before carving.
- Serve immediately.

Servings: 8

Nutritional Information Per Serving:
Energy: 135 Kcal
Carbohydrates: 1.2 g
Net Carbs: 1.2 g
Fats: 5 g
Protein: 34 g

10.   Turkey Meatballs

Ingredients

- 6 oz ground turkey
- 1/3 cup coconut flour
- 1/2 cup chopped red bell pepper
- 1/2 cup chopped white onion
- 18 oz passata, low-carb and sugar-free

Instructions

- Mix all of the ingredients, apart from the tomato passata, together in a bowl, and season with salt and ground black pepper.
- Shape the mixture into meatballs, you should get 18 to 20 balls.
- Grease a 4-quart slow-cooker with a non-stick cooking spray and cover the bottom evenly with the passata.
- Place the meatballs in the sauce, cover and seal the slow-cooker with its lid.
- Set the cooking timer for 6 to 8 hours, and allow to cook at a low heat setting.
- Serve the meatballs warm, with the sauce drizzled on top.

Servings: 3

Nutritional Information Per Serving:
Energy: 128 Kcal
Carbohydrates: 1 g
Net Carbs: 1 g
Fats: 2 g
Protein: 9 g

Low-Carb Seafood Recipes

1. Poached Salmon

Ingredients

- 4 salmon fillets
- 1 medium-sized white onion, peeled and sliced
- 1 lemon, sliced
- 1/2 cup chicken broth
- 1 cup water

Instructions

- Place the ingredients in a 4-quart slow-cooker, holding back 4 lemon slices to garnish.
- Cover and seal slow-cooker with its lid, then set the cooking timer for 2 hours. Allow to cook at a high heat setting.
- Serve hot, with the sauce alongside.

Servings: 4

Nutritional Information Per Serving:
Energy: 133 Kcal
Carbohydrates: 1.7 g
Net Carbs: 0.96 g
Fats: 3.9 g
Protein: 22.9 g

2. Apricot Salsa Salmon

Ingredients

- 8 oz wild salmon fillet
- 3 tablespoon apricot spread, sugar-free
- 1/4 cup Salsa Verde,

Instructions

- Grease a 4-quart slow-cooker with a non-stick cooking spray and place the salmon fillet into it.
- Stir the remaining ingredients together, and spread this mixture over the salmon.
- Cover and seal the slow-cooker with its lid, and set the cooking timer for 1 to 1 1/2 hours. Allow to cook at a low heat setting or until salmon is cooked through.
- When done, flake the salmon fillet with forks and serve. This dish can be eaten hot or cold.

Servings: 2

Nutritional Information Per Serving:
Energy: 173.1 Kcal
Carbohydrates: 4.6 g
Net Carbs: 4.2 g
Fats: 6.3 g
Protein: 27.1 g

3. Garlic Shrimps

Ingredients

- 8 oz shrimps, peeled, deveined and rinsed
- 3 teaspoons minced garlic
- 1 teaspoon smoked paprika
- 1/4 teaspoon crushed red pepper flakes
- 2 tablespoons soy sauce

Instructions

- Mix all the ingredients apart from the shrimps, and season with 1 teaspoon salt and ¼ teaspoon ground black pepper.
- Place in the slow-cooker, then seal the slow-cooker with its lid.
- Set the cooking timer for 30 minutes, allowing it to cook at a high heat setting.
- Gently add the shrimps, and allow to cook for a further 15 minutes or until shrimps are cooked through and opaque.
- Garnish with parsley and serve.

Servings: 4

Nutritional Information Per Serving:
Energy: 210 Kcal
Carbohydrates: 2 g
Net Carbs: 2 g
Fats: 12 g
Protein: 23 g

4. Orange Fish Fillets

Ingredients

- 4 salmon fillets
- 4 oranges, segmented
- 1 tablespoon Dijon Mustard
- 1 tablespoon orange juice and a large piece of orange rind, sugar-free
- 1/2 cup apple cider vinegar

Instructions

- Mix the vinegar, mustard, orange juice, orange rind, salt and ground black pepper together.
- Cut out 4 aluminum foil pieces, big enough to wrap around each fish fillet, then place a salmon fillet on each aluminum foil piece.
- Spread prepared vinegar mixture over the top and top with the orange segments.
- Gently fold aluminum foil over each fillet and form a parcel by crimping the edges.
- Place these parcels into a 4-quart slow-cooker, then cover and seal slow-cooker with its lid.
- Set the cooking timer for 2 hours, allowing it to cook at a high heat setting.
- Remove the aluminum packets with a tongs, uncover fillets, flake with forks, and serve.

Servings: 4

Nutritional Information Per Serving:
Energy: 120 Kcal
Carbohydrates: 2.7 g
Net Carbs: 2.3 g
Fats: 6.8 g
Protein: 19.1 g

5. Fish with Tomatoes

Ingredients

- 6 oz cod
- 1 white onion, peeled and sliced
- 1 1/2 teaspoon minced garlic
- 1 can diced tomatoes
- 1/4 cup chicken broth

Instructions

- Season the cod with a pinch of salt and pepper and red chili flakes.
- Mix the remaining ingredients together, and place into a 4-quart slow-cooker.
- Gently place the seasoned cod on top, then cover and seal the slow-cooker with its lid, setting the cooking timer for 1 to 1 1/2 hours.
- Allow to cook at a high heat setting or until fish is cooked through.
- Serve warm.

Servings: 2

Nutritional Information Per Serving:
Energy: 220 Kcal
Carbohydrates: 3.64 g
Net Carbs: 2.5 g
Fats: 6.7 g
Protein: 34.8 g

6. Shrimp Scampi

Ingredients

- 16 oz shrimps, peeled, deveined and rinsed
- 1 tablespoon minced garlic
- 2 tablespoon melted unsalted butter or olive oil
- 1 tablespoon lemon juice
- 3/4 cup chicken broth

Instructions

- Mix all of the ingredients together, apart from the shrimps.
- Season with salt and black pepper, and place in a 4-quarts slow-cooker.
- Add shrimps, mixing the ingredients gently together.
- Cover and seal slow-cooker with its lid, and set the cooking timer for 2 1/2 hours. Allow to cook at a low heat setting or until shrimps are cooked through.
- Garnish with cheese and serve immediately.

Servings: 4

Nutritional Information Per Serving:
Energy: 256 Kcal
Carbohydrates: 2.1 g
Net Carbs: 2 g
Fats: 14.7 g
Protein: 23.3 g

7. Clam Chowder

Ingredients

- 1 ¼ lb baby calms, with juice
- 1 cups each of chopped onion and chopped celery
- 1 teaspoon dried thyme
- 2 cups coconut cream, full-fat
- 2 cups chicken broth

Instructions

- Grease a 4-quarts slow-cooker with a non-stick cooking spray and place all ingredients inside.
- Season with a pinch of salt and ground black pepper.
- Cover and seal the slow-cooker with its lid, and set the cooking timer for 4 to 6 hours. Allow to cook at a low heat setting or until cooked through.
- Serve immediately.

Servings: 6

Nutritional Information Per Serving:
Energy: 391 Kcal
Carbohydrates: 5 g
Net Carbs: 5 g
Fats: 29 g
Protein: 27 g

8. Lemon Pepper Tilapia with Asparagus

Ingredients

- 6 Tilapia fillets
- 1 bundle of asparagus
- 4 teaspoons lemon-pepper seasoning
- 3 tablespoons unsalted butter
- 1/2 cup lemon juice

Instructions

- Cut out 6 aluminum foil pieces, each big enough to wrap a Tilapia fillet.
- Place each fillet on a piece of aluminum foil, then evenly sprinkle with lemon-pepper seasoning and lemon juice.
- Top each fillet with a knob of butter, then place the asparagus spears on top.
- Gently fold the aluminum foil over each fillet, and form a parcel by crimping the edges.
- Place these parcels into a 4-quart slow-cooker, then cover and seal the slow-cooker with its lid.
- Set the cooking timer for 3 hours, allowing to cook at a high heat setting or until fillets are cooked through.
- Remove the parcels with a tongs, then unwrap the fillets, flake the fish with forks, and serve.

Servings: 6

Nutritional Information Per Serving:

Energy: 320 Kcal
Carbohydrates: 19 g
Net Carbs: 10 g
Fats: 24 g
Protein: 60 g

9. Pesto Salmon with Vegetables

Ingredients

- 2 salmon fillets
- 8 oz fresh green beans, trimmed
- 4 teaspoons basil pesto
- 10 cherry tomatoes, quartered
- 3 lemons, juiced

Instructions

- Grease a 4-quart slow-cooker with a non-stick cooking spray and place the cherry tomatoes and green beans inside.
- Rub the salmon fillets with salt and black pepper, and place on top of the vegetables.
- Mix together the pesto and the lemon juice, then drizzle over the salmon fillets and vegetables.
- Cover and seal slow-cooker with its lid, and set the cooking timer for 2 to 3 hours.
- Allow to cook at a low heat setting or until fillets are cooked through.
- Serve fish fillet and vegetables with cooked cauliflower rice.

Servings: 2

Nutritional Information Per Serving:

Energy: 435 Kcal
Carbohydrates: 9 g
Net Carbs: 5 g
Fats: 26 g
Protein: 33 g

Low-Carb Pork Recipes

1. Cranberry Pork Roast

Ingredients

- 2 lb pork shoulder, on the bone
- 1/4 cup dried minced onion
- 8 oz cranberry sauce, low-carb and sugar-free
- 1/4 cup raw honey

Instructions

- Grease a 4-quart slow-cooker with a non-stick cooking spray and place the pork shoulder inside.
- Sprinkle with minced onion, then drizzle with honey and top with the cranberry sauce.
- Cover and seal slow-cooker with its lid, then set the cooking timer for 5 to 6 hours.
- Allow to cook at a high heat setting, or until pork is cooked through and tender.
- Carve the meat and serve, with the cooking juices alongside.

Servings: 4

Nutritional Information Per Serving:
Energy: 391.3 Kcal
Carbohydrates: 19.2 g
Net Carbs: 17 g
Fats: 25 g
Protein: 37 g

2. Pulled Pork

Ingredients

- 1 small pork roast, quartered
- 1 white onion, peeled and chopped
- 1 green pepper, sliced and chopped
- 3 tablespoons dry Italian seasoning

Instructions

- Grease a 4-quart slow-cooker with a non-stick cooking spray and place the pork roast inside it.
- Sprinkle with the Italian seasoning, then top with the onion and pepper.
- Cover and seal slow-cooker with its lid, then set the cooking timer for 5 to 6 hours.
- Allow to cook at a high heat setting, or until pork is cooked through and tender.
- Shred the meat with forks and then serve between two roasted mushrooms caps, with cream cheese.

Servings: 2

Nutritional Information Per Serving:
Energy: 214 Kcal
Carbohydrates: 4 g
Net Carbs: 4 g
Fats: 12 g
Protein: 21 g

3. Balsamic Pork Tenderloin

Ingredients

- 16 oz pork tenderloin
- 1/2 cup balsamic vinegar
- 2 tablespoon coconut aminos
- 1 tablespoon Worcestershire sauce
- 2 teaspoons minced garlic

Instructions

- Grease a 4-quart slow-cooker with a non-stick cooking spray, place the pork inside, and sprinkle with the garlic.
- Mix the remaining ingredients in a bowl, along with ½ teaspoon red pepper flakes.
- Pour this mixture over the pork, and seal the slow-cooker with its lid.
- Set the cooking timer for 4 to 6 hours, and allow to cook at a low heat setting.
- Transfer the pork to a serving platter, drizzle with 1/2 cup of cooking liquid and carve to serve.

Servings: 8

Nutritional Information Per Serving:
Energy: 188 Kcal
Carbohydrates: 1.3 g
Net Carbs: 1.3 g
Fats: 5.8 g
Protein: 30.3 g

4. Honey-Mustard Barbecue Pork Ribs

Ingredients

- 1 ½ lb pork ribs, boneless
- 2 teaspoons garlic-and-herb seasoning blend
- 2 oz Dijon mustard
- 2 oz soy sauce
- 4 oz raw honey

Instructions

- Place a large skillet pan over a medium heat, and grease with a dash of olive oil.
- Cook the ribs in batches, until they are nicely browned on all sides.
- Drain the grease and transfer the browned pork ribs to a 4-quart slow-cooker.
- Mix the remaining ingredients together in bowl.
- Pour this mixture over pork ribs, then cover and seal slow-cooker with its lid.
- Set the cooking timer for 4 to 5 hours, and allow to cook at a high heat setting.
- Transfer the pork ribs to a serving platter, skim any fat from the sauce, and drizzle the sauce over the chops.
- Serve hot.

Servings: 8

Nutritional Information Per Serving:
Energy: 342 Kcal
Carbohydrates: 18.4 g
Net Carbs: 15.7 g
Fats: 20.2 g
Protein: 22.3 g

5. German Style Pork Stew

Ingredients

- 1 lb boneless pork chops
- 1 can diced tomatoes
- 1 1/2 cups cubed rutabaga
- 1 1/2 teaspoons dried oregano
- 4 cups chicken broth

Instructions

- Grease a 4-quarts slow-cooker with a non-stick cooking spray and place all ingredients inside.
- Season with 1 teaspoon salt, ½ teaspoon ground black pepper and 1/2 teaspoon ground cumin.
- Cover and seal slow-cooker with its lid, then set the cooking timer for 3 1/2 to 4 hours, allowing it to cook at a high heat .
- Serve immediately.

Servings: 8

Nutritional Information Per Serving:
Energy: 352 Kcal
Carbohydrates: 8.53 g
Net Carbs: 6.31 g
Fats: 14.6 g
Protein: 44.5 g

6. Pork Chops with Broccoli

Ingredients

- 6 oz pork chops
- 1 medium-sized red onion, peeled and chopped
- 2 cups broccoli florets
- 4 tablespoons soy sauce
- 1 tablespoon sesame seeds

Instructions

- Grease a 4-quarts slow-cooker with a non-stick cooking spray and place the pork, onion, soy sauce and 1/2 cup water inside.
- Cover and seal slow-cooker with its lid, and set the cooking timer for 7 hours, allowing to cook at a high heat setting.
- Add the broccoli and continue cooking for 20 to 30 minutes or until the broccoli is tender.
- Serve the meat, garnished with sesame seeds, with the vegetables and the sauce alongside.

Servings: 6

Nutritional Information Per Serving:
Energy: 293.9 Kcal
Carbohydrates: 5.7 g
Net Carbs: 4.9 g
Fats: 15 g
Protein: 33.4 g

7. Lemon and Coconut Pork

Ingredients

- 1 lb pork, trimmed
- 1 teaspoon minced garlic and 1 tablespoon grated ginger
- 3 heads bok choy, halved
- 2 red bell peppers, cored and diced
- 1 tablespoon grated coconut

Instructions

- Grease a 4-quarts slow-cooker with a non-stick cooking spray and place all of the ingredients inside, apart from the coconut.
- Stir in 1 cup beef broth, then seal the slow-cooker with its lid.
- Set the cooking timer for 4 to 6 hours, allowing it to cook at a high heat setting.
- Add the coconut and allow to continue cooking for a further 20 minutes.
- Garnish with more shredded coconut and serve immediately.

Servings: 4

Nutritional Information Per Serving:
Energy: 288Kcal
Carbohydrates: 12.8 g
Net Carbs: 7.1 g
Fats: 13.6 g
Protein: 29.9 g

8. Green Chile Pork

Ingredients

- 1 lb pork shoulder roast
- 2 Serrano Chili peppers
- 1/2 cup chopped cilantro
- 1 white onion, peeled and chopped
- 8 oz green salsa

Instructions

- Grease a 4-quart slow-cooker with a non-stick cooking spray and place the onion at the bottom.
- Rub the pork with salt and ground black pepper, then place on top of the onions.
- Pour the salsa over the pork, then sprinkle with cilantro and add the chili peppers.
- Cover and seal slow-cooker with its lid, and set the cooking timer for 8 hours, allowing it to cook at a low heat setting.
- Transfer the pork to a serving platter.
- Serve the meat with the sauce and the vegetables alongside

Servings: 6

Nutritional Information Per Serving:

Energy: 400 Kcal
Carbohydrates: 5 g
Net Carbs: 4.1 g
Fats: 21 g
Protein: 22.5 g

9. Teriyaki Pork Tenderloin

Ingredients

- 12 oz pork tenderloin
- 2 teaspoons minced garlic
- 1/4 cup raw honey
- 1/2 cup teriyaki sauce, low-carb and sugar-free
- 1 cup chicken broth

Instructions

- Place a large skillet pan over medium-high heat, grease the pan with a little olive oil, and add the pork tenderloin.
- Allow to cook for 15 minutes, turning as required until it is nicely browned on all sides.
- In the meantime, prepare teriyaki sauce by whisking together remaining ingredients.
- Transfer the browned pork tenderloin into a 4-quart slow-cooker, and pour in prepared teriyaki sauce.
- Cover and seal the slow-cooker with its lid, and set the cooking timer for 4 hours, allowing it to cook at a low heat setting
- When cooked, transfer pork tenderloins to a serving platter and allow to rest for 5 minutes.
- Drizzle with the sauce and serve.

Servings: 6

Nutritional Information Per Serving:
Energy: 330.2 Kcal
Carbohydrates: 11.6 g
Net Carbs: 11.3 g
Fats: 15.9 g
Protein: 33.4 g

10.   Sweet and Sour Pork

Ingredients

- 10 oz pork, trimmed and diced
- 2 bell peppers, de-seeded and diced
- 1 tablespoon grated ginger
- 1/4 teaspoon xanthan gum
- 1 1/2 cup sweet and sour sauce, low-carb and sugar-free

Instructions

- Place a large skillet pan over medium-high heat, grease the pan with a little olive oil, and add the pork.
- Allow to cook for 2 to 3 minutes per side, or until nicely golden brown on all sides.
- Transfer the browned pork to a 4-quart slow-cooker and pour in the sweet and sour sauce.
- Cover and seal slow-cooker with its lid, then set the cooking timer for 3 to 4 hours, allow it to cook at a low heat setting.
- Stir in the xanthan gum and the diced peppers.
- Continue cooking for a further 20 minutes at a high heat setting, until sauce has reduced to the desired thickness, and the peppers are tender.

- Garnish with sesame seeds and serve.

Servings: 4

Nutritional Information Per Serving:
Energy: 467 Kcal
Carbohydrates: 21.4 g
Net Carbs: 3.9 g
Fats: 32 g
Protein: 49 g

11.   Barbecue Pork Ribs

Ingredients

- 2 lb pork ribs
- 3 cups hot barbecue sauce, low-carb and sugar-free

Instructions

- Set the oven to 400 degrees F and allow to preheat.
- In the meantime, rub the pork ribs with salt and ground black pepper and place on a baking sheet in a single layer.
- Place the baking sheet into the preheated oven, and allow to bake for 30 minutes, or until nicely golden brown.
- Drain the grease from the pork ribs and place the ribs in a 4-quart slow-cooker.
- Top with barbecue sauce and toss to coat.
- Cover and seal slow-cooker with its lid, then set the cooking timer for 6 to 8 hours, allowing it to cook at a high heat setting.
- Serve immediately.

Servings: 6

Nutritional Information Per Serving:

Energy: 414 Kcal
Carbohydrates: 2 g
Net Carbs: 2 g
Fats: 36 g
Protein: 18 g

Low-Carb Vegetarian Recipes

1. Green Beans

Ingredients

- 16 oz green beans, fresh or defrosted frozen
- 1 white onion, peeled and diced
- 1 teaspoon minced garlic
- 14 fl oz chicken broth
- 1/3 cup grated Parmesan cheese

Instructions

- Place a medium-sized skillet over a medium heat, add 2 tablespoons of olive oil and allow to heat.
- Add the onion and the garlic, and cook gently for 5 minutes, until soft.
- Transfer this mixture to a 4-quart slow-cooker, and add the remaining ingredients, apart from the cheese.
- Season with salt and black pepper, stir until mixed, then cover and seal the slow-cooker with its lid.
- Set the the cooking timer for 4 hours, and allow to cook on a a low heat setting.
- Sprinkle with the cheese and continue to cook for a further 20 minutes, or until the cheese has completely melted.
- Serve immediately.

Servings: 4

Nutritional Info:
Energy: 120 Kcal
Carbohydrates: 4.3 g
Net Carbs: 2.8 g
Fats: 9.9 g
Protein: 4.8 g

2.   Eggplant Salad

Ingredients

- 1 red onion, peeled and sliced
- 2 red bell peppers, de-seeded and sliced
- 1 eggplant, quartered and sliced
- 1 can chopped tomatoes
- 1 tablespoon smoked paprika

Instructions

- Grease a 4-quart slow-cooker with a non-stick cooking spray, and place all of the ingredients inside.
- Season with salt and ground black pepper and stir until all ingredients are well-combined.
- Cover and seal the slow-cooker with its lid, and adjust the the cooking timer for 7 to 8 hours, allowing it to cook on a a low heat setting.
- Serve with cooked cauliflower rice.

Servings: 6

Nutritional Info:
Energy: 130 Kcal
Carbohydrates: 8.9 g
Net Carbs: 6 g
Fats: 9.4 g
Protein: 2.1 g

3.   Cauliflower and Cheese

Ingredients

- 1 large cauliflower head, split into florets
- 1/4 teaspoon garlic powder
- 3 tablespoons melted butter
- 1 cup shredded cheddar cheese
- 4 oz sour cream

Instructions

- Grease a 4-quart slow-cooker, place the cauliflower florets inside, and season with salt and black pepper.
- Seal the slow-cooker with its lid, and adjust the the cooking timer for 2 1/2 hours, allowing to cook at a a low heat setting.
- Stir the remaining ingredients together, then pour over the cauliflower florets.
- Allow to continue to cook for a further hour.
- Serve immediately.

Servings: 6

Nutritional Info:
Energy: 199 Kcal
Carbohydrates: 5 g
Net Carbs: 3 g
Fats: 17 g
Protein: 8 g

4.   Thai Yellow Curry

Ingredients

- 2 teaspoons minced garlic and 1 tablespoon grated ginger
- 1/2 cup cherry tomatoes, halved
- 2 teaspoons Thai yellow curry paste
- 2 teaspoons fish sauce and 3 teaspoons soy sauce
- 1 can full-fat coconut milk, unsweetened

Instructions

- In a 4-quart slow-cooker, place all the ingredients apart from the tomatoes.
- Stir until mixed, then seal the slow-cooker with its lid.
- Set the the cooking timer for 7 hours and allow to cook at a low heat setting.
- Add the tomatoes to the mixture, and allow to cook for a further hour.
- Garnish with cilantro, and serve with cauliflower rice.

Servings: 6

Nutritional Info:
Energy: 185 Kcal
Carbohydrates: 9 g
Net Carbs: 7 g
Fats: 29 g
Protein: 9.4 g

5.   Vegetable Curry

Ingredients

- 1 cup cauliflower florets
- 2 medium-sized sweet potatoes, peeled and cubed
- 3 tablespoons red curry paste
- 3 tablespoons soy sauce and 2 teaspoon Sriracha sauce
- 1 can full-fat coconut milk, unsweetened

Instructions

- Place the cauliflower florets and sweet potatoes in a 4-quart slow-cooker.
- Mix the remaining ingredients together in a separate bowl, and season with a pinch of salt and a tablespoon of brown sugar.
- Pour this mixture over the vegetables, then seal the slow-cooker with its lid.
- Set the the cooking timer for 4 hours, and allow to cook at a a low heat setting.
- Garnish with cilantro and basil and serve with cauliflower rice.

Servings: 4

Nutritional Info:
Energy: 205 Kcal
Carbohydrates: 12 g
Net Carbs: 4.8 g
Fats: 13.5 g
Protein: 9 g

6.   Pepper-Jack Cauliflower

Ingredients

- 1 cauliflower head, cut into florets
- 2 tablespoons unsalted butter, melted
- 4 oz Pepper Jack cheese, shredded
- 4 oz cream cheese, full-fat
- 1/4 cup whipping cream, full-fat

Instructions

- Grease a 4-quart slow-cooker with a non-stick cooking spray, and add all the ingredients apart from the Pepper Jack cheese.
- Stir until combined, then cover and seal slow-cooker with its lid.
- Set the the cooking timer for 3 hours and allow to cook at a a low heat setting.
- Stir in the Pepper Jack cheese and continue cooking for a further 30 minutes.
- Garnish with basil and serve.

Servings: 6

Nutritional Info:
Energy: 272 Kcal
Carbohydrates: 6.28 g
Net Carbs: 4.27 g
Fats: 21.29 g
Protein: 10.79 g

7.Cauliflower Mash

Ingredients

- 2 cauliflower heads, cut into florets
- 6 fl oz chicken broth
- 3 tablespoons unsalted butter, melted
- 4 oz sour cream
- 1/2 teaspoon garlic powder

Instructions

- Place the chicken broth and the cauliflower florets in a 4-quart slow-cooker.
- Cover and seal slow-cooker with its lid, adjust the cooking timer for 3 hours, and allow to cook at a high heat setting.
- Mash the florets using a stick blender, then stir in remaining ingredients and season with a pinch of salt and ground black pepper.
- Garnish with parsley and serve.

Servings: 8

Nutritional Info:
Energy: 145 Kcal
Carbohydrates: 4 g
Net Carbs: 2.78 g
Fats: 11 g
Protein: 6 g

8.   Mushroom Stroganoff

Ingredients

- 1 ½ lb mushrooms, sliced
- 1 white onion, sliced
- 2 teaspoons minced garlic and 2 teaspoons smoked paprika
- 1 tablespoon sour cream
- 1 cup vegetable stock

Instructions

- Grease a 4-quart slow-cooker with a non-stick cooking spray, and place all of the ingredients inside, apart from the sour cream.
- Cover and seal slow-cooker with its lid, and adjust the cooking timer for 4 hours, allowing to cook at a high heat setting.
- Stir in the sour cream, and season with a pinch of salt and ground black pepper.
- Garnish with parsley and serve.

Servings: 2

Nutritional Info:

Energy: 116 Kcal
Carbohydrates: 11 g
Net Carbs: 7.3 g
Fats: 12 g
Protein: 3 g

9.   Vegetable Fajitas

Ingredients

- 3 bell peppers, deseeded and sliced
- 3 white onions, sliced
- 1 can tomatoes
- 2 green chilies
- 3 teaspoons ground cumin and 1 teaspoon dried oregano

Instructions

- Grease a 4-quart slow-cooker with a non-stick cooking spray and add all ingredients to it.
- Season with 3 teaspoons red chili powder and 1/2 teaspoon garlic salt.
- Cover and seal the slow-cooker with its lid, and adjust the cooking timer for 4 to 6 hours.
- Allow to cook at a a low heat setting.
- Garnish with cilantro to serve.

Servings: 4

Nutritional Info:
Energy: 51 Kcal
Carbohydrates: 5.8 g
Net Carbs: 3.5 g
Fats: 6.5 g
Protein: 1.7 g

10. Cauliflower and Pea Risotto

Ingredients

- 12 oz cauliflower rice
- 1 cup green peas
- 2 tablespoons heavy cream
- 1/2 cup grated parmesan cheese
- 1 1/2 cups chicken broth

Instructions

- Grease a 4-quart slow-cooker and add the cauliflower rice and chicken broth.
- Season with garlic salt and ground black pepper, and stir to combine.
- Cover and seal slow-cooker with its lid, and adjust the cooking timer for 3 hours.
- Allow to cook at a a low heat setting.
- Stir in the peas and the cheese, and continue cooking for a further hour.
- Stir in the heavy cream to serve.

Servings: 6

Nutritional Info:
Energy: 245 Kcal
Carbohydrates: 7.57 g
Net Carbs: 5.2 g
Fats: 19.68 g
Protein: 8.18 g

Low-Carb Soup Recipes

1. Cream of Sweet Potato Soup

Ingredients

- 24 oz sweet potatoes, peeled and chopped
- 1 red onion, peeled and chopped
- 2 celery stalks, chopped
- 5 cups chicken stock
- 1 cup full-fat coconut milk, unsweetened

Instructions

- Grease a 4-quart slow-cooker and add all the ingredients to it, apart from the coconut milk.
- Season with salt and ground black pepper, and stir to combine.
- Cover and seal slow-cooker with its lid, and adjust the cooking timer for 6 hours.
- Allow to cook at a a low heat setting.
- Puree the soup using a stick blender until smooth, then stir in the coconut milk.
- Continue cooking for 30 minutes and then ladle soup into warm bowls to serve.

Servings: 4

Nutritional Info:
Energy: 163 Kcal
Carbohydrates: 11.5 g
Net Carbs: 8.5 g
Fats: 13.9 g
Protein: 4.6 g

2.   Taco Soup

Ingredients

- 1lb ground sausage
- 2 cans chopped tomatoes
- 2 tablespoons of taco seasonings
- ½ lb cream cheese
- 4 cups chicken broth

Instructions

- Place a large skillet over a medium heat, pour in a tablespoon of olive oil, then add the ground sausage.
- Allow to cook for 7 to 10 minutes, until the meat is nicely browned.
- In the meantime, place the remaining ingredients into the slow-cooker and stir until well mixed.
- Drain the grease from the meat and add to the slow-cooker.
- Stir all ingredients together until well-mixed, then cover and seal the slow-cooker with its lid.
- Adjust the cooking timer for 4 hours, and allow to cook at a a low heat setting.
- Garnish with cilantro and cheese and serve.

Servings: 8

Nutritional Info:

Energy: 547 Kcal
Carbohydrates: 5 g
Net Carbs: 4 g
Fats: 20 g
Protein: 33 g

3.   Creamy Cauliflower Soup

Ingredients

- 1 cauliflower head, cut into florets
- 1 teaspoon minced garlic
- 4 oz grated cheddar cheese
- 8 oz heavy cream
- 4 cups chicken stock

Instructions

- Grease a 4-quart slow-cooker and add the cauliflower florets, garlic, and stock.
- Season with salt and ground black pepper, and stir until mixed.
- Cover and seal slow-cooker with its lid, and adjust the cooking timer for 4 to 6 hours, allowing to cook at a a low heat setting.
- Stir in the cream and the cheese, and blend until smooth using a stick blender.
- Serve immediately.

Servings: 6

Nutritional Info:
Energy: 290 Kcal
Carbohydrates: 6 g
Net Carbs: 4 g
Fats: 25 g
Protein: 10 g

4.   Greek Lemon Chicken Soup

Ingredients

- 4 chicken breasts, skinless
- 4 cups spaghetti squash
- 1/4 cup parsley, chopped
- 1/3 cup lemon juice, fresh
- 3 eggs
- 10 cups chicken stock

Instructions

- Season the chicken with salt and ground black pepper, and add to a 4-quart slow-cooker.
- Add the spaghetti squash, parsley, and chicken stock, and stir until well-mixed.
- Cover and seal the slow-cooker with its lid, and adjust the cooking timer for 4 to 5 hours, allowing to cook at a low heat setting.
- Remove the chicken from the soup, and shred using forks.
- Return the shredded chicken to the slow-cooker.
- Beat the egg and the lemon juice together in a bowl, then add one cup of the hot broth mixture, stirring continuously.
- Add this heated lemon mixture to the slow-cooker, and stir until combined.
- Adjust the seasoning, and ladle the soup into warmed bowls to serve.

Servings: 6

Nutritional Info:

Energy: 289 Kcal
Carbohydrates: 9 g
Net Carbs: 4 g
Fats: 15 g
Protein: 33g

5.   Zuppa Toscana Soup

Ingredients

- 6 oz ground Italian sausage
- 8 oz cauliflower florets
- 3 cups chopped kale
- 2 fl oz chicken stock
- ½ cup heavy cream

Instructions

- Place a large skillet over a medium heat, pour a tablespoon of olive oil onto the pan, and add the ground sausage.
- Cook for 7 to 10 minutes, until nicely browned.
- Drain off the fat, and transfer the meat to the slow-cooker.
- Add the cauliflower florets, kale, and chicken stock, and season with salt, ground black pepper, and red pepper flakes.
- Stir until mixed, then cover and seal slow-cooker with its lid.
- Adjust the cooking timer for 8 hours and allow to cook at a a low heat setting.
- Gently stir in the cream, and serve immediately.

Servings: 6

Nutritional Info:

Energy: 246 Kcal
Carbohydrates: 7 g
Net Carbs: 3.3 g
Fats: 19g
Protein: 15 g

6. No Noodles Chicken Soup

Ingredients

- 1 whole chicken
- 4 cups mixed broccoli, cauliflower florets, and carrots, chopped into bite-sized pieces
- 16 celery stalks
- 6 cups water

Instructions

- Cut half of the celery into 4-inch pieces and place in the slow-cooker.
- Place the chicken on top, and season salt and ground black pepper.
- Pour in the broth, and seal the slow-cooker with its lid.
- Adjust the cooking timer for 8 to 10 hours, and allow to cook at a a low heat setting.
- Remove the chicken, remove the meat from the bones.
- Dice the remaining celery, and add to the slow-cooker along with the chicken and the mixed vegetables.
- Allow all of the ingredients to continue cooking for 1 to 2 hours at a high heat setting.
- Adjust the seasoning, then ladle the soup into warmed serving bowls.

Servings: 10 servings

Nutritional Info:
Energy: 201 Kcal
Carbohydrates: 4 g
Net Carbs: 3 g
Fats: 10 g
Protein: 27 g

7.Cream of Asparagus Soup

Ingredients

- 12 oz asparagus, ends trimmed
- 1 cup chopped white onion
- 2 teaspoons Vegeta seasoning
- 3/4 cup heavy cream
- 4 cups chicken broth

Instructions

- Place all of the ingredients apart from the cream in a 4-quart slow-cooker, and stir gently until mixed.
- Cover and seal slow-cooker with its lid, and adjust the cooking timer for 6 to 8 hours, allowing it to cook at a a low heat setting.
- Blend the soup until smooth using a stick blender.
- Gently stir in the cream and serve.

Servings: 4

Nutritional Info:

Energy: 350 Kcal
Carbohydrates: 7.7 g
Net Carbs: 4.8 g
Fats: 32.3 g
Protein: 8.7 g

8.   Pumpkin Soup

Ingredients

- 4 cups chopped butternut pumpkin
- 1/2 teaspoon minced garlic and 1 tablespoon grated ginger
- 1 1/2 teaspoon mild curry powder
- 1/2 teaspoon red chili powder
- 7 cups chicken stock

Instructions

- Place all of the ingredients in a 4-quart slow-cooker, and stir until mixed.
- Cover and seal slow-cooker with its lid, then adjust the cooking timer for 4 1/2 hours and allow to cook at a a low heat setting.
- Blend the soup until smooth using a stick.
- Garnish with watercress and serve.

Servings: 6

Nutritional Info:
Energy: 254 Kcal
Carbohydrates: 10.4 g
Net Carbs: 9.1 g
Fats: 18.9 g
Protein: 12.7 g

9. Shrimp Fajita Soup

Ingredients

- 6 oz shrimp, peeled and deveined
- 1 red bell pepper, de-seeded and diced
- 1 white onion, peeled and sliced
- 2 tablespoons and 1 teaspoon fajita seasoning
- 3l chicken broth

Instructions

- Place all of the ingredients apart from the shrimps in a 4-quart slow-cooker.
- Stir until mixed, then cover and seal the slow-cooker with its lid.
- Adjust the cooking timer for 4 hours, and allow to cook at a low heat setting.
- Add the shrimps, and continue to cooking for 20 to 30 minutes at a high heat setting until the shrimps are opaque.
- Ladle the soup into warmed serving bowls to serve.

Servings: 4

Nutritional Info:

Energy: 292 Kcal
Carbohydrates: 14 g
Net Carbs: 7.3 g
Fats: 15.5 g
Protein: 22 g

10. Red Bell Pepper and Basil Soup

Ingredients

- 4 red bell peppers, deseeded and halved
- 5 garlic cloves, peeled and sliced
- 1/3 oz basil
- 1 teaspoon salt
- 1 cup heavy cream

Instructions

- Place the bell pepper, garlic, basil, and salt in a 4-quart slow-cooker, and mix gently.
- Cover and seal the slow-cooker with its lid, then adjust the cooking timer for 3 hours, and allow to cook at a high heat setting.
- Puree the mixture using a stick blender, then gently fold in the cream.
- Ladle the soup into warmed bowls to serve.

Servings: 4

Nutritional Info:

Energy: 228 Kcal
Carbohydrates: 8 g
Net Carbs: 6.5 g
Fats: 21.5 g
Protein: 3.2 g

Low-Carb Snack Recipes

1. Pizza

Ingredients

- 8 slices of pepperoni
- 1 lb ground beef, cooked
- 1 cups spinach and your favorite pizza toppings
- 1 jar pizza sauce, unsweetened
- 2 cups shredded mozzarella cheese

Instructions

- Combine the ground beef and pizza sauce together in a bowl, and spread this mixture on the bottom of a 4-quart slow-cooker.
- Top with the spinach leaves, and then with 8 pepperoni slices.
- Add your favorite toppings, such as sliced mushrooms, chopped green bell pepper, chopped tomatoes and minced garlic.
- Cover with the mozzarella cheese, then seal the slow-cooker with its lid.
- Set the cooking timer for 4 to 6 hours, and allow to cook at a low heat setting.
- Allow the pizza cool slightly before slicing to serve.

Servings: 8

Nutritional Info:
Energy: 487 Kcal
Carbohydrates: 7.6 g
Net Carbs: 5.6 g
Fats: 37 g
Protein: 30 g

2.   Granola

Ingredients

- 1/2 cup each of raw hazelnuts, almonds, and walnuts
- 1 cup each raw pumpkin seeds and sunflower seeds
- 1 cup shredded coconut, unsweetened
- 1 teaspoon vanilla extract, unsweetened
- 1/2 cup agave syrup

Instructions

- Grease a 4-quarts slow-cooker with melted coconut oil, then add the vanilla extract, the nuts, seeds, and shredded coconut, stirring all of the ingredients well together.
- Whisk together the agave syrup, a pinch of salt and a ½ teaspoon of ground cinnamon, and drizzle over nut and seed mixture.
- Cover and seal slow-cooker with its lid, then adjust the cooking timer for 2 hours, and allow to cook at a low heat setting, stirring every half an hour.
- When the granola is nicely browned, transfer it to a baking pan, spread it evenly, and allow to cool completely before serving.

Servings: 12

Nutritional Info:
Energy: 337 Kcal
Carbohydrates: 8.7 g
Net Carbs: 5.2 g
Fats: 31.6 g
Protein: 7.9 g

3. Cheese Artichoke Dip

Ingredients

- 14 oz artichoke hearts, drained and chopped
- 1 red bell pepper, diced
- 16 oz grated mozzarella cheese
- 1 cup grated parmesan cheese
- 1 cup mayonnaise

Instructions

- Place all the ingredients apart from the cheese in a 4-quart slow-cooker, and stir until mixed.
- Cover and seal the slow-cooker with its lid, then adjust the cooking timer for 3 hours, allowing it to cook at a low heat setting.
- Gently stir in the cheese, and continue cooking for a further hour.
- Allow to cool before serving.

Servings: 8

Nutritional Info:

Energy: 386 Kcal
Carbohydrates: 8.9 g
Net Carbs: 5.5 g
Fats: 29 g
Protein: 2.1 g

4.   Cajun Chicken Stuffed Avocado

Ingredients

- 3 avocados, stone removed and halved
- 3 chicken thighs
- 2 teaspoons Cajun seasoning
- 1/4 cup mayonnaise and 2 tablespoons sour cream
- 2 tablespoons lemon juice

Instructions

- Place the chicken into a 4-quart slow-cooker, sprinkle with the Cajun seasoning, and pour in 2 cups water.
- Cover and seal the slow-cooker with its lid, then adjust the cooking timer for 8 hours, allowing it to cook at a low heat setting.
- Remove the chicken, and shred it, using forks, and discarding the bones.
- Season the chicken with salt and cayenne pepper, add the remaining ingredients, apart from the avocado, and stir until well-combined.
- Chop up half of each avocado into small pieces, and stir into the chicken mixture.
- Fill each remaining avocado half with the prepared chicken mixture.
- Serve a stuffed avocado half to each person, with some chicken and avocado salad alongside.

Servings: 3

Nutritional Info:
Energy: 638 Kcal
Carbohydrates: 21 g
Net Carbs: 5.4 g
Fats: 50.6 g
Protein: 34.5 g

5.   Parmesan Chicken Wings

Ingredients

- 24 chicken wings
- 4 teaspoons minced garlic
- 1 tablespoons dried parsley
- 2 cups grated Parmesan cheese

Instructions

- Place the chicken wings in a 4-quart slow-cooker.
- Place 1 cup of parmesan cheese, the garlic and parsley in a separate bowl, mixing well.
- Season with salt and black pepper, then pour onto the chicken wings, tossing the wings to coat them well.
- Cover and seal slow-cooker with its lid, then adjust the cooking timer for 2 ½ to 3 hours, allowing to cook at a high heat setting.
- In the meantime, switch on the grill and allow to heat.
- Transfer the chicken onto a large baking sheet, lined with a parchment sheet, and sprinkle with the remaining cheese.
- Place the baking sheet under the grill, and allow to grill for 5 minutes, or until cheese has completely melted and the chicken wings are crispy.
- Serve immediately.

Servings: 4

Nutritional Info:
Energy: 223 Kcal
Carbohydrates: 0.8 g
Net Carbs: 0.3 g
Fats: 21.7 g
Protein: 25.1 g

6.   Tomato and Feta Cheese Dip

Ingredients

- 1 can tomatoes
- 1/2 white onion, peeled and diced
- 2 1/2 cups mixed basil, oregano and parsley leaves
- 1/4 cup red wine
- 8 oz cubed feta cheese

Instructions

- Place a medium-sized skillet over medium heat, add 2 tablespoons oil and allow to heat.
- Add the onion, and allow to cook for 5 to 7 minutes, until the onion is soft.
- Stir in 1 teaspoon of minced garlic and a pinch of crushed red pepper.
- Continue to cook for another 2 minutes, then add the wine.
- Stir continuously until the wine evaporates, then stir in the herbs and tomatoes.
- Transfer this mixture into a 4-quart slow-cooker, add the cheese, and season with salt and ground black pepper.
- Cover and seal the slow-cooker with its lid, then adjust the cooking timer for 3 hours and allow to cook at a high heat setting.
- Allow to cool before serving.

Servings: 8

Nutritional Info:
Energy: 182 Kcal
Carbohydrates: 7 g
Net Carbs: 5 g
Fats: 10 g
Protein: 4 g

7.Chocolate Fondue

Ingredients

- 2 1/2 oz chopped chocolate, chopped and unsweetened
- 1/3 cup Swerve Sweetener, powdered
- 1/2 teaspoon vanilla extract, unsweetened
- 1 cup full-fat coconut cream

Instructions

- Grease a 4-quart slow-cooker with a non-stick cooking spray and add all ingredients to it.
- Stir until combined, then cover and seal slow-cooker with its lid.
- Adjust the cooking timer for 2 hours and allow to cook at a low heat setting until smooth.
- Serve as a dip with mixed fruit.

Servings: 8

Nutritional Info:
Energy: 154 Kcal
Carbohydrates: 3.7 g
Net Carbs: 2.3 g
Fats: 14.87 g
Protein: 1.8 g

8.   French Onion Dip

Ingredients

- 3 white onions, peeled and thinly sliced
- 1/2 teaspoon garlic powder
- 2 cups sour cream
- 1/2 cup mayonnaise
- 2 tablespoons melted coconut oil

Instructions

- Add the onions and coconut oil to a 4-quarts slow-cooker.
- Cover and seal the slow-cooker with its lid, and adjust the cooking timer for 7 to 9 hours.
- Allow to cook at a low heat setting, stirring occasionally until the onion has caramelized.
- Leave the onion to cool until it reaches room temperature, then transfer them to a bowl and add the remaining ingredients.
- Season with salt and ground black pepper, mix all ingredients well together.
- Serve as a dip with vegetables.

Servings: 8

Nutritional Info:
Energy: 522 Kcal
Carbohydrates: 12.8 g
Net Carbs: 11 g
Fats: 51.7 g
Protein: 3.5 g

9.   Queso Dip

Ingredients

- 8 oz cream cheese, cubed
- 8 oz Monterey Jack cheese
- 12 oz Salsa Verde

Instructions

- Place all of the ingredients in a 4-quart slow-cooker and stir until mixed.
- Cover and seal the slow-cooker with its lid, and adjust the cooking timer for 2 1/2 hours.
- Allow to cook at a low heat setting, stirring every half hour.
- Puree the mixture with a stick blender, allow to cool, and serve with chopped vegetables.

Servings: 8

Nutritional Info:
Energy: 171 Kcal
Carbohydrates: 3 g
Net Carbs: 2.7 g
Fats: 14 g
Protein: 6 g

10. Cauliflower Hummus

Ingredients

- 3 cups cauliflower florets
- 5 garlic cloves, peeled
- 1 1/2 tablespoons tahini paste
- 2 tablespoons olive oil
- 3 tablespoons lemon juice

Instructions

- Place the cauliflower florets in a 4-quart slow-cooker, add 3 garlic cloves and 1/4 cup water, and season with a pinch of salt.
- Cover and seal the slow-cooker with its lid, and adjust the cooking timer for 3 to 4 hours.
- Allow to cook at a low heat setting.
- Pulse the cauliflower mixture with a stick blender until smooth.
- Add the remaining ingredients and pulse again with a stick blender until smooth.
- Adjust the seasoning, drizzle with olive oil and serve with chopped vegetables.

Servings: 8

Nutritional Info:
Energy: 141 Kcal
Carbohydrates: 7 g
Net Carbs: 3.5 g
Fats: 14 g
Protein: 2 g

Conclusion

The slow-cooker makes low-carb cooking easy and very convenient. With just a little preparation, you can have a hassle-free and tasty low-carb dish anytime you want. Even the carb lovers will enjoy these scrumptious dishes!

Take a low-carb diet challenge and make a positive change in your life!

Made in the USA
San Bernardino, CA
17 February 2018